Education of Scheduled Castes

Education of Scheduled Castes

S.K. Yadav

Commonwealth

Education of Scheduled Castes

ISBN : 81-7169-130-7

Edition : 2024

Published by :
COMMONWEALTH PUBLISHERS (P) LTD.
4831/24, Govind Lane,
Ansari Road, Darya Ganj,
New Delhi - 110002
Ph. : 23272541, 23242541
e-mail : commonwealthpublishers2016@gmail.com

Distributed by :
ARJUN PUBLISHING HOUSE
4831/24, Govind Lane,
Ansari Road, Darya Ganj,
New Delhi - 110002
Ph. : 23272541, 23242541
e-mail : arjunbooks2001@gmail.com

Laser Typesetting by :
Dimple Computers
Delhi

Printed at :
Milan Enterprises
Delhi

TO

MY PARENTS

Whose honesty, sincerety and hardwork have always been a source of inspiration to me.

Preface

Research is an important tool for bringing out social, economic and educational changes and reforms in the individual, the society and the nation. In the society like ours, there are various types of hinderances blocking progress of weaker sections of society. Due to these, various sections of the society have been ignored and remain backward since ages. The scheduled castes, a large chunk of the population, is one of them and have been suffering for the last so many decades. They are a miserable lot in the society. They could not make progress despite various efforts made by government and non-governmental agencies, because the efforts were not in right direction and could not made scientifically and systematically. Research in this area can answer these questions and can also provide held to ameliorate their suffering lot.

In this book, an attempt has been made to highlight various problems, gaps and disparities through research studies. The book has seventeen chapters. These chapters have been divided into sections. Section—A has reviewed various research studies available in the area. Section—B has highlighted some of the significant research studies. The last chapter on 'Research Perspective' has suggested some of the significant areas which have been touched upon so far and also have an important place in this area. In this regard, a model experimental research design has also been discussed here.

Besides this, I express my thanks to the students, teachers and parents who were involved and cooperated me in conducting the research studies which are presented in this book. I also owe we a sense of gratitude to Prof. N.K. Jangira, Prof. G.L. Arora and Dr. (Mrs.) Saroj Yadav, all from NCERT, New Delhi, who not only provided me guidance and help but also brought to the stage of publication. My friend, Mr. Anand Singh Yadav, who has always been moving spirit to complete this task, also deserves my thanks and gratitude.

This book will be very useful to the researchers, scholars, administrators, planners and field functionaries for implementing the various policies and programmes for the total development of scheduled castes.

S.K. YADAV

List of Tables

Contents

SECTION B : RESEARCH STUDIES

1

Introduction

According to 1981 consus, the scheduled caste population in India was 10.4 crores which constituted 16 per cent of the total population. This large chunk of the population has been suffering since ages and they have been named in different forms like shudras, untouchables, depressed classes, harijans etc; with the passage of time. But their conditions remained pathetic and they continued to suffer socially, educationally and economically. In 1935, the Government of India passed an Act and named as Scheduled Castes Act in which certain castes, races and tribes were put together. The Government provided some incentives for improving their conditions but besired result could not be achieved. After independence the list of scheduled castes was revised in 1950 and some more avenues were provided for minimising the gaps between scheduled castes and the general castes. Substantial funds were allocated in the National Five Year Plans for ameliorating the conditions of the scheduled castes. The Constitution of the country also includes a special article 46 which states "The state shall promote with special care the educational and economic interests of the weaker sections of the people and shall protect them from special injustice and all forms of exploitation". The centre and state government implemented this article by providing different schemes and provisions for the welfare of the scheduled castes but the achievements are far from satisfactory. If we look to the education, the literacy rates of scheduled castes were 14.67% and 21.38% against 29% and 36.6% of the general population according to 1971 and 1981 census. This reveals wide gap between the literacy of the two. The same is the case of enrolment ratio. During 1986-87 the enrolment ratio of scheduled caste students from classes I to V in the age group 6-11 years was 84.8 per cent againt the 95.9 percent of general population, which was about 10% more in comparison to scheduled castes. The same is the position at middle level in classes 6th to 8th in the age group 11 to 14 years. The enrolment ratio of the scheduled caste was 40% and that of the general caste was 53.1%. The above disparity could not be removed dispite various efforts of the government. It means various efforts made by the government and other agencies were not in right direction and could not bring fruitful results. What were the reasons for not bringing out the desired result? Why this joint venture of the government and the other welfare agencies failed? Why the funds allocated for the welfare for scheduled castes have been the wasted? Why different schemes for them did not work properely? Where does the fault lie ? How can it be improved? Research can only provide answers to these questions. The schemes and benefits are being provided to the scheduled castes without considering the consequences and implications of research. NPE, 1986 has also placed lot of emphasis on research in the education of scheduled castes to ameliorate their conditions and bringing them at par with general castes. Constant micro-planning and verification to ensure that the enrolment, retention and successful completion of courses by SC students do not fall at any stage, and provision of remedial courses to improve their prospects for further education and employment (NPE P. 4.5 (III). In the area of research and development, and education in science and technology, special measures will be taken to establish network arrangements between different institutions in the country to pool their resources and participate in projects of national importance (P. 3.9).

Research in the universities will be provided enhanced support and steps will be taken to ensure its high quality. Suitable mechanism will be set up by the U.G.C. for coordinating research in the universities, particularly in thrust areas of science and technology, with research undertaken by other agencies. An effort will be made to encourage the setting up of national research facilities within the university system, with proper forms of outonomous managements (5.32). Research in Indology, the huminities and social sciences will receive adequate support. To fulfil the need for the synthesis of knowledge, inter-disciplinary research will be encouraged. Efforts will be made to delve into India's ancient fund of knowledge and to relate it to contemporary reality. This effort will imply the development of facilites for the intensive study of sanskrit and other classical languages (5.33).

Besides this, various Committees and Commissions have emphasised the imporance of research in the development of human life, removing the inequalities and disparities among the different section of the society, and bringing advancement and modernisation. John W. Best (1959) emphasized that the secret of our cultural development has been research, pushing back the areas of ignorance by discovering new truths which in turn lead to better ways of doing things and better product. The University Education Commission (1950) also laid special emphasis on research. Human civilisation has derived great benefits from the efforts of specialists who have penetrated ever more deeply into the secrets of nature and the motives and processes of human behaviour, individual and social. To a constantly increasing extent modern life is the outcome of research. To quote white—head "a progressive society depends on its inclusion of three groups scholars, discoverers, inventors". While the scholars rediscover the past and set before us ideals of wisdom, beauty and goodness, discoverers findout new truths and inventors apply them to pre sent needs. The universities are the chief agencies for producing these types of men who will fuse progressive activities into an effective instrument. Universities are responsible as much for extending the boundaries of knowledge as for the training of citizens in fact, the advancement of knowledge is a necessary condition of the continued vitality of their teaching for unless a study is rooted in research, it will die. Although the argument for research must rest upon the broad basis of its value in the intellectual progress of mankind, in India research has become a practical necessity for the continued progressive growth of our national life—in a critical appraisal and conservation of the best in our ancient indigencous calture (arts, history, philosophy and literature) as well as in modernizing and improving our agriculture, industry and public health. In the Huminities, research concern itself mainly with the past history of man—the history of his thought as well as of his experiences, the understanding of a man as a whole and the integration of the past with the present; while in natural sciences research takes the form of searching out the undiscovered properties of nature and their application to the material needs of mankind. Humanistic research increases our Knowledge of human nature and enables us to form correct judgements. Faced as we are with difficult and economic problems, on the correct solution of which the very existence of our nation depends, we need all the equipment we can get from a sober evaluation of the ideal and material motives which influence human action as well as from a full acquaintance with economic laws and their working. As regards Natural Sciences and Technology, even the man in the strect appreciates the fruits of research when he makes use of an automobile, an aeroplane, the radio, the cinema, the penicillin and the refrigerator. The last war and the difficult post war conditions have forced even our administrators to think of scientific research which can enable us to grow more food on land and harvest more of it from the sea, find substitutes for petrol and coal, produce better breeds of milch cattle and conquer malaria, plague and other diseases. (University Education Commission 1948-49).

When the man in the street speaks of research, he generally thinks of research in natural sciences, but educated men cannot undervalue the mutual relations of the different departments of knowledge, the primary philosophical truth to which we cannot attach a materialistic value, and all that respective Knowledge which is in the largest sense is called History. If we develop a community with a large amount of material knowledge, power and energy, with more or less of an absence of widespread influences of humanities, it will be in a perilous condition is a crisis for lack of that enlarged knowledge and philosophical thinking, and refinement of symphathies and testes which we owe to the humanities. Only by a combination of sciences and humanites can a true conception of civilisation survive. (UEC 1948-49).

Humanistic research has a greater advantage over scientific research in that it is comparatively inexpensive. It does not need extensive laboratories and a costly equipment of instruments, but it does not need some equipment. Its main need is a first class library. Although our library resources are poor and universities are not generally well stocked in books and manuscripts, and are in need of generous grants, still they are ample resources in our country for research in Languages and Literature, classical and modern, Philosophy, Religion, History and Fine Arts. Humanities have another advantage in that teachers and students of these subjects have comparatively greater leisure as compared with teachers and students of Sciences, who have to spend long hours in their laboratories (UEC, 1950).

The Secondary Education Commission emphasised that the Training College should in essence be not merely a college for teachers trainig, but an institution for undertaking research in all aspects of pedagogy. The staff of the college should be such as would be capable of devoting some of their time to research in curricular and extra-curricular activities, general administration modern trends of pedagogy and also from time to time in research to evaluate results of the particular method of training adopted in different schools. For this purpose every training college desiring to conduct educational research should have under its control an experimental or demonstration school besides the practising school (SEC, 1952-53).

Education Commission (1964-66) laid stress on the importance and function of research at the university level and highlighted the powerful impact that it has on the entire national life. Some major aspects can be summarised as follows :

(i) Production of Researchers : The university system is the central place for the identification of research talent. It produces almost all the researchers of the country. It gives them basic training in research. Thus, the quality of national research depends to a very large extent on the quality of university research.

(ii) Performance of Research : The universities in educationally advanced countries but not in India to-day) do a very considerable portion of natural research, both in quantity and variety. The top leaders of science of a country are generally in the universities or work in close association with them.

(iii) Quality of Teaching : Engagement in research work is a major pre-condition for creative teaching and stimulation of creativity.

(iv) Producing Teachers : Since the universities produce their future teachers, and also for secondary schools, a developed research atmosphere in the universities has a direct bearing on the entire character and quality of teachers, and through them it influences the identification and development of their students.

(v) Training of Leaders: Leaders and decisionmakers in nearly all fields of national life are generally the products of the university system. A major takes of the universities is to enable the country's future leaders to develop interest in the development of a scientific attitude in tackling the problems they are called upon to face in their work.

(vi) Consultative Function : Through its research function, the university staff can and does provide advisory and consultative services to other institutions engaged in research, production, decision making etc. This should be vigorously encouraged in our country.

(vii) Research Policy : In most countries it is the universities which supply the majority of advisory personnel for research policy bodies, including committees advising at the highest level of government.

(viii) Scientific Tradition : The university staff play a key role in the development and improvement of the scientific tradition of the country, and in the organisation and development of a socially aware and active scientific community. The university staff perform this function through their contacts and communication with each other, and with scientists outside the university. Through individual contacts and through students societies the teachers help to develop scientific tradition and proper norms of behaviour in the students—the scientific community of the future. Scientific societies of staff and students in university departments and colleges play an important role in promoting research interest and creativity in youth.

(ix) International Contacts : The academic bodies at a national level consisting largely of university scientists play a major role in promoting international contacts and understanding which often extend beyond the domain of science.

(x) Government and Universities: A healthy relationship between university and the Government is of vital importance in ensuring a balanced and fruitful interaction between Government and science generally.

The above discussion makes it clear that research is an important tool for bringing about social, economic and educational changes and reforms in the individual, the society and the nation. It also minimises the gaps between the lower and the uppercastes of the society. No doubt, the scheduled castes, the weaker section of the society, have been suffering since ages but research attention has improved their status in the society to some extent. Various research studies have been conducted on social educational and economic aspects of the scheduled castes. The reports of Commissioner for Scheduled Castes and tribes present data every year on different facets of their life and make recommendations to improve their lot. The different universities and national institutions have been doing researches at masters and doctoral level for ameliorating their condition S. Patwardhan (1966) noted in his study that the Holar, the very low in hierarohy of the Scheduled Castes raised their social status to the level of the Chamar. T.R. Singh (1969) revealed that social distance between the higher castes and scheduled castes has narrowed down. The scheduled castes were seeking to align with the higher castes. Andre Beleille (1967) finds that the sanskritization affects culture of castes in the lower and middle regions of the castes. The scheduled castes are now learning more and more to make increasing use of political action to bargain for better position in society Eleanor Zelliot (1970) described the process by which Mehars in Maharashtra ameliorated their social conditions through political means. Dr. Ambedkar played key role in this regard. He (1946) claimed that the shudras of the Indo-Aryan society were Kshatriyas. Singh (1982) revealed that in urban areas the Hindu temples, dharamshalas and religious bathing ghats are being used by the scheduled castes. Jha (1972) in his study did not find significant difference on untouchability in the attitude of the higher and lower castes. Aggarwal (1974) showed that the scheduled castes have gained social equality and raised their status due to protective laws, education and franchise. Naik (1972) found that education is related to untouchability. The educated had negative attitude towards untouchability. Besides these, Yadav (1983) conducted an awareness study about educational schemes. He found that the parents who were aware about the educational schemes utilised more benefits as compared to those who were unaware. The aware parents' children were found more educated, in a better occupation, and a better economic status as compared to others. Like this many researchers have conducted many investigations on the education, social, economic and plitical aspects of scheduled castes which has proved that it has helped a lot in improving the conditions of the scheduled castes. Research findings bring to light the loop holes of different aspects of the problems and also suggest the systematic steps for solving the problems. In this book an attempt to has been made to highlight the researches conducted on the scheduled castes so that their conditions can be ameliorated and the existing gap between the scheduled castes and the higher castes can be bridged. They can also be saved from different types of evils and disabilities prevalent in the society since ages.

This book consists of seventeen chapters and is divided into two sections. The Section—A which includes eight chapters, focusses on the research reviews of different studies. The section—B highlights the several revealing findings of seven research studies on scheduled castes. The *First chapter* gives the outline of the book. The *Second chapter* presents a review of studies on untouchabiltity. It has been studied in the perspective of education, economic and socialaspects etc. The *Third chapter* on Educational Wastage Amongst Scheduled Castes reveals the incidence of drop-out and stagnation and their causes. The remedial solutions in form of action points have also been suggested in this chapter. The fourth chapter on Awareness of Scheduled caste's about Educational Schemes covers the studies related to parents and their children awareness about educational schemes. The *Fifth chapter* reviewed the research studies related to utilisation of educational benefits and incentives. The *Sixth chapter* is on Constraints and Utilisation of Educational Schemes. It highlights the problems related to utilisation of educational schemes by the scheduled castes. The *Seventh chapter* entitled

Facilitators of Implementation of Educational Schemes, enumerates the action points for solving the problems encountered in the utilisation of educational benefits. The *Eighth chapter* reviews the studies related to Motivational Tendencies, Intelligence, Academic Achievement and Adjustment among scheduled castes. The *Ninth chapter* focusses the reviews of the researches on attitude, self-concept and aspiration level among the scheduled castes. The *Tenth chapter* is on Demographic Profile of Scheduled Castes Families. It discusses the educational, economic, occupational and political status of the scheduled caste families. The *Eleventh chapter* entitled Cognitive and Motivational Level of the Scheduled Castes and Non-scheduled Castes Students compared the intellectual level of the two categories of the students. It also compares the motivational tendencies between the scheduled castes and non-scheduled caste students. The *Twelfth chapter* presents a study related to vocational anxiety of the scheduled caste students. It has also been studied from point of view of their sex, place of living and the academic achievement.

The *Thirteenth chapter* gives the glimpse of perception of the teachers towards educational schemes for scheduled castes children. It also highlights the consequences of the perception of the teachers. The *Fourteenth chapter* is on Attitude of Teacher Trainees Towards Games and Sports. It gives the degree of variation of attitude among scheduled caste students and explanins as to how they are inclired towards games and sports. The *Fifteenth chapter* on Attitude of Teacher Trainees Towards Teaching focusses the inclination of the scheduled caste students towards teaching profession and how it differs among males and females? The *Sixteenth chapter* is on Parental and Students' Awareness About Educational Schemes. This study has studied the antecedants of awarenees and also the consequences of awareness about educational schemes. The last and the *Seventeenth chapter* is no Research Perspective. This chapter gives the implications for action and the gaps in the past and recent researches. The suggestions for minimising the gaps have been discussed. The various areas of researches on scheduled castes have also been pinpointed.

In the conclussion, this chapter has discussed the general education of scheduled castes in comparison to non-scheduled castes. How can the gaps between the two be bridged in the context of NPE, 1986? How can the research investigations help in removing the disparaties between the two? what are the important recommendations for researches by various committees and commissions? These question have been discussed in the present chapter. Lastly a brief outline of all the seventeen chapter has been presented. The next section—A focusses the reviews of researches conducted about the scheduled castes.

Section—A : Research Overview

This section comprises the reviews of researches conducted in the area of education for the scheduled castes. The research overviews include the studies of untouchability, educational wastage. awareness of educational benefits, utilisation of educational schemes, constraints in utilisation of schemes, motivational tendencies, intelligence, academic achievement, adjustment, attitude, self concept and aspiration level among scheduled castes. These studies not only highlight the present state of a affairs of scheduled caste's education but may also help in improving their lot. Besides, these studies give further guidelines for more researches which can be of immense help to plan education for disadvantaged sections of our society.

2

Untouchability Among Scheduled Castes

The scheduled castes are scattered all over the country. The only thing they share in common is poverty and social disabilities arising from the untouchability among these people. Untouchability is a multifaceted concept. It is associated with scheduled castes in different degrees and forms. Different kinds of social, educational and occupational distances are kept by Hindu castes dispite legal safeguards provided by our constitution after independence while dealing with scheduled castes. In this chapter an attempt has been made to highlight the various kinds of untouchability faced by the scheduled castes and also focussed the various attempts made by the government and voluntary agencies to improve their status in the saciety.

Social

Social disabilities hamper the creativity and aspiraion of the scheduled castes and also bring the inferiority complex among these people. In the study of Upadhyay (1981), it was found that the harijans were debarred from entering temples, on the other hand these untouchables aspired to attain this privilege. Most of the higher caste people had not favoured social relations like marrigages of their children with harijans, combined get together, draw water from a common well and entry into religious places etc. whereas most of the lower caste people had no institutions about social intercourse with upper caste men. Singh (1982) also supported the findings of this study. But in the urban areas the Hindu temples, dharamshalas and religious bathing ghats are being used by the scheduled castes due to the mixed population, even then there is feeling of insult and fear of old beliefs and traditions in the minds of the scheduled caste people (Doshi, 1974). However, Maurya (1974) reported in his study that no discrimination was found against the scheduled caste in the past.

Occupation

The traditional occupation encourage untouchability between the scheduled castes and the non-scheduled castes. The families of the scheduled castes mostly follow the traditional occupation and did not gain any significant access to the occupational mobilization accelerated by the democratic process (Upadhayay, 1981). In this regard, Lynch (1968) also studied the case of Jatav—a caste of leather workers in the city of Agra. Being an untouchable caste, they are segregated occupationally and residentially. They occupy the low lying areas of the city. This case has been making streneous efforts at social climbing since the begining of this country.

Education

The practices of untouchability are being observed in the educational institutions also. Khurana (1980) reported that the main hurdle in the way of education of scheduled caste was the practice of untouchability. Naik (1971) also felt that wastage and stagnation was higher among the scheduled caste students than those of the other communities on account of stigma of untouchability, besides poverty, defective system of admission and lack of special attention to these institutions. Parental attitude have not been very much encouraging and supportive towards education. The report of Commissioner of Scheduled Castes and Scheduled Tribes (1969) pointed out that the prejudicial atmosphere against the so-called untouchable was equally responsible for compelling them to leave their education in the middle. The practice is not only found in schools and colleges but also in the attached hostels and their messes. Maurya (1976) supported the above findings and reported that the traditional disabilities of these people are still prevailing highly in the educational institutions and the so-called untouchables are treated as such even by their teachers who are the makers of the future of the students.

Economic

Economic factor affects the rate of untouchability Upadhayay (1981) found that the untouchable population in general was found to be underpaid and belonged to the low earning group. In this direction a new struggle has started between haves and have nots among the Harijan themselves. Uutouchability also continues to persist and requires a fresh approach to be eradicated completely (Aggarwal,1974). In addition to this it was found that the level of aspiration of the untouchables to improve the economic status was found to be very high as even the illiterate parents had shown a clearcut liking for jobs in administrative and professional fields (Upadhyay, 1981). However, the government has made various attempts to improve the economic status of scheduled castes by providing scholarships, reservation for jobs and admission in educational institutions even then these incentives have served to reinforce the separate identity of these castes rather than to integerate with rest of the society (Ramaswamy, 1964).

Attitude

Attitude of higher caste towards scheduled caste plays an important role in increasing and decreasing the rate of untouchability. In his study Jha (1972) did not find significant differences among scheduled castes in the attitude of different groups when classified by age, education, income, marital status and previous residence. This may be due to the inadequate size of the samples in different groups. Also enough literate persons with different characteristics from among the scheduled castes were not available for assessing the effect of education and age etc. However, scavengers the most favourably inclined than the Jatav in their attitude towards abolition of untouchability. Again urban students have shown a more favourable attitude than correspondence rural students. Ssimilarly persons in the government service are more favourably inclined than the persons in the shoemaking business. On the other hand persons in the government service donot differ in their attitude from those in private service probably because majority belongs to scavengers class. This seems to be the effect of caste among the untouchables indicating untouchability among the untouchables. Further those who object to Brahmin or dislike the scheduled castes are less favourably inclined than those who object to none. Two of the Jatav objected to living in the neighbourhood of scavengers showing comparatively less favourable attitude than those who did not object to anyone. Besides, there is untouchability among the untouchables themselves. The harijan treat scavengers as the lowest caste and agriculturist (Machigars) among the harijans as the higest caste. There are ten castes in the area covered in the study and they are almost endogamous groups where intermarriages and intermingling are restricted to a great extent and only the institution of untouchability is binding them as one group. The notion of untouchablity is not only restricted to Harijans but many hindus, when they are in state of purity like to observe untouchability with other caste as well. The institution of untouchability and the practice of purity and pollution have roots in the ideas of purity and pollution (Kedetotad, 1978). Inspite of this Silveesten (1963) also analysed the intercaste relations in a multicaste village in the Tanjore district. He has noted the radical changes in the status of untouchables in that village. Even now all the higher caste avoid scheduled caste quarter while the letter are barred from the Brahmin streets and from using wells frequented by other castes. The barber, carpenter and washerman donot serve them. They have priests of their own caste in their shrines.

Action Points

In order to raise the status, the harijans tried to change the name of their group. Traditionally they were called as Asprashya, Atin, Antyaja and Holeya, now they like to adopt a sanskritized name The words like adijana, adi-hindus have been coined in the local as well as at the national level. Some of the leaders among the harijans thought that the word Harijan itself showed different group of untouchables and assumed to adopt such names as 'Adi Jana' or "Adi Hindus" to show that they were the original inhabitants of the country.

Some of them have tried to embrace other faiths like christianity, Islam, Buddhism, etc: to change their status. But since conversion has not improved their social status, there is no incentive for it. Expecially among the lower classes of Harijans, Change of religion is disliked and condemned. Among them the notion of Karma has a greater influence. So they realised that modernization and urbanization have some times protected the Harijans from the evils of untouchability. The status and conditions of Harijans of Karnataka are alightly different from those of Harijans elsewhere in India. As veerashaivism did convert them into their own religion during the twelfth century and the veerashaivas of Karnataka fell a prey to the institution of untouchability in due course of time as the Hindus, the impact of lingayats on Harijans of Karnataka is found in their ritual, daily life and in their society. The Harijans of Karnataka mostly belong to veerashaiva faith and many of Harijans caste are named after saints (Sharanas) who were veerashaivas and who born as aspharashyas. Some of the saints like Kakkayya, Channayya, Haralayya had a high status. The woman saints of Asprashyas was equal to high born woman saints of veerashaivism. During the century, Basaveshwara, a veerashaiva reformer went to the extent of arranging marriage between Brahmin girl and a shudra boy. The impact of such instances is still alive. The entire life and practices of Harijans follow the Hindu religion like a shadow and the Harijans never accepted any other faith or religion. In deed it is difficult for the caste

Hindus to conduct their ceremonies and daily life without Harijans (Kedetotad, 1978).

Another factor which leads to minimise the practice of untouchability is education which certainly will bring the improvement in the status of the scheduled castes. Traditionallv education was confined to upper caste people only. The British government in 1923 issued instruction against discrimination and non-admission of the depressed classes students in schools and also emphasised that no grants would be paid to any aided educational institutions if depressed class students were not admitted in schools. Though their presence in schools was disliked by their social superiors but after issuence of the instructions the admission and sitting in classroom was liberalised and the rate of discrimination was alio minimised. Social status recognition and the basis of social status are the most important concerns of the untouchables. Downtrodden and subjugated, as they were by the higher caste, on the basis of their low caste membership, the untouchables try to seek new basis of status hierachy. The data show that respondents from urban, sub-urban and rural areas equally agree that education should be the criterion of determining one's social status (Toha& Srivastava, 1971). Aggarwal (1974) showed in his study that scheduled caste have gained social equality and raised their status due to protective laws, education and franchise.

The respondents belonging to the urban areas are more prone to such qualities of personality which are characteristic of the modern dynamic individual. Most of urbanities believe in doing one's own work and participation inthe social activities as the most important characteristic of human personality whereas the rural people like the virtues of benevolence as the most important characteristic of individual personality. Suburban people show a liking for both modern as well as traditional attributes of personality but their learning is more towards the traditional characteristic of benevolence (Toha and Srivastava 1971).

Aiyappan (1966) in his study of Mayur, a Kerala village has described the changing status of the scheduled castes. The caste he is dealing with here is that of Irava. The Iravas began an agitation to abolish distance pollution as far back as 1911 and a decade latter they started an agitation for temple entry. The latter movement gained the support of Mhatma Gandhi. Now-a-dyas no member of a superior caste can order a member of the lower caste to go off the road to avoid being polluted by the latter. The taboos against the untouchables have disappeared. The Iravas are now set on the road to progress. They are now getting education and are growing cash crops which give them more money. The Iravas are also regarded as advanced.

Besides this, Alaxander (1968) reported the changes in the status of Pulaya Harijans of Kerala. Traditionally they were at the bottom of the caste hierarchy. They have gained greater economic independence through education and through the enactment of laws prohibiting discrimination against them, the have attained a highest status in the society. This higher status is evidenced by changes in behaviour pattern, made of dress, common eating and drinking or in other words, by the near disappearance of untouchability.

Another study of Naik (1972) clearly showed that the education is positively related to attitude towards abolishing untouchability. The higher the level of education the more favourable the attitude and vice verca. And this is true in the case of the education of the respondent' father who, perhaps, play an important role in the attitude formation of their children towards the practice of untouchability. Except, for business class, the higher the occupational level, the more favourable is the attitude towards untouchables. Sahay (1975) stressed that education plays significant role in eradicting the untouchability. He advocated that education at all levels should be given free and compulsory. Meritorious students should be given free foreign and higher education.

The education of scheduled caste woman had resulted

in bringing about profound changes in their attitude towards marriages. The educated scheduled caste woman believed in having their marriage arranged with her consent. Although they did not seem to reject outright all the traditional customs, the followed them only to a limit. Due to contact with higher castes, the custom of dowry had been introduced among the educated scheduled caste people which the educated scheduled caste women disapproved of. This has created new problems of education, the educated scheduled caste women felt that they had attained a status in her family which was not at all recognised in the past (Doshi, 1974). Due to higher education, the scheduled caste women achieved a high status, which was unknown in their family and community. As more as 90% of the respondents felt that education made them realise that they should change their way of life. A considerable percentage of the respondents expressed their dislike for the traditional habits and customs. The respondents reported that education was helpful in reducing the caste barrier and therefore the scheduled caste women could easily adjust themselves to higher class people. Thus it was due to education that the scheduled caste members had been accepted at least in the urban society on par with the members of the higher classes. With the apportunity for education, the scheduled caste women had emerged as a minority class struggling to secure new jobs that would enable them to raise their status. At first the educated scheduled caste women entered the world of employment as strangers and outsiders. However, it could be seen that the traditional outlook particularly towards the educated scheduled caste women's taking up various jobs had undergone considerable changes and the attitude of the higher caste colleagues were found to be satisfactory.

Education improved the status not only in urban areas but in rural areas also. Toha & Srivastava (1971) showed that untouchables from urban areas perceived personality development through education as the most important aim of education. The student of the sub urban areas are of the opinion that education provides social status and a good job, respectively. The rural students also perceived education mainly as a avenue of economic gains whereas these from urban areas are more concerned with the aesthetic and moral aspects of education. The study too showed that students from all areas are in favour of higher education. This clearly indicates that they are in position to understand the importance of education for their offspring. But the students of rural areas, comparatively are not in favour of higher education for their offspring. The majority of the respondents from the urban and sub-urban believed that modern education is instrumental in achieving the ends of life (Toha and Srivastava, (1971).

The above discussion has reflected the different dimensions of untouchability which are associated with it in different forms and affect the scheduled caste people in the society. These various factors affecting untouchability have been analysed and put into systematic order in this chapter. The action points for minimising the rate of untouchability have been discussed here. Various efforts made by government and voluntery organisation were also highlighted which helped the scheduled caste people in improving their status in the society. Lastly it is also concluded that education played an vital role in eradicating the untouchability whether it is due to social or economic or any other reason.

3

Educational Wastage Amongst Scheduled Castes

There is no denying the fact that education is an important instrument for the total development of the child's personality. But in a caste ridden and hierarchical society like India's, access to educational opportunities is unequal and unjust. The so called higher castes with better economic power had the sole monopoly in the field of education during preindependence days and the lower castes, especially Scheduled Castes were denied the educational facilities. However, after independence, special measures were proposed in our constitution for the education of the scheduled castes and liberal plan allocations were made under different five year plans to improve the lot of Scheduled Castes. Inspite of this, there is glaring disparity in the education of scheduled castes and non-scheduled castes. To find out the causes of disparity, various committees have been set up and research studies have been conducted. Most of these studies have concluded that wastage is the main reason for hindrance in the way of progress of the scheduled castes.

The term 'wastage' has been defined in different ways. UNESCO (1968) defines that educational wastage includes two main components (1) grade repetition, which refers to pupils who are held back in the same grade and do the same work as in the previous year, and (2) dropout or withdrawal from a school cycle before its competion. However the most common veiw of 'wastage' implied premature withdrawal of a child from school cycle before completing the last grade of the stage of education in which he is studying. For the removal of wastage in education, the causes of wastage have to be investigated so that this chronic disease can't create read blocks in the path of progress of education of scheduled castes. In the present paper, about fifty studies dealing with dropouts among scheduled castes have been reviewed.

Incidence of Drop-outs

The incidence drop-outs among scheduled caste varies from one situation to another situation. It has been found that rate of wastage is more in scheduled castes than in non-scheduled castes which may be due to many reasons including stigma of untouchability (Sharma and Sapra, 1969; Naik, 1971; Pimpley, 1974; Singh, 1974; Nayer, 1975; Chitnis, 1976; Dantawala, 1976; Mehta, 1976; Chitnism, 1977 and Yadav, 1984).

Some students have indicated the incidence of wastage at various school stages. Chandrasekhraiah (1969) found that largest dropout is in the classes I and II, while Adiseshiah (1974), Kariekar (1975) and Mishra (1978) reported that the percentage of detention was highest at the primary stage (I-V classes). But some studies have concluded that wastage exist at the middle stage or after 8th class (Chauhan, 1375; Maurya, 1976).

Another category of studies points out the difference in wastage of education in relation to demographic variables of age and sex. Pimpley (1975) and Shah (1976) found that the largest number of dropout was of male than female students while Singh (1969) and Gore (1974) found that wastage of education is not less than 80% in lower age groups particulary school—age children (6-14 years).

Another set of studies refers to wastage of education in relation to place of living. Chaudhary (1970), Gore (1974) and Mehta (1976) found that the children belonging to rural areas have higher rate of dropout than the children belonging to urban areas while Pimpley (1978) reported that the urban children had a higher rate of dropout than rural children. Another category of the studies on wastage of education refers to income bracket of the parents belonging to scheduled castes. These studies concluded that the parents whose income is less than Rupees 1500 per annuam have more dropout children in the family as compared to the parents having more income. (Kariekar, 1975; Rastogi, 1976 and Yadav 1984).

Causes of Wastage

There are a number of social, educational, occupational and economic factors which affect the wastage of education among scheduled castes. Therefore, the causes of wastage of education as revealed by different studies have been broadly classified under the four categories mentioned above :

Economic

In most of the studies poverty and economic backwardness of the family has been one of the most important causes contributing to wastage in education. This specific cause has been interpreted in the form of consequence of poverty i.e. lack of good clothing, shelter, medical facilities, stationery and cost of education which compelled them to give up their studies (Chandrasekharaiah, 1969; Singh, 1969; Naik, 1971; Shah, 1972: Dubey, 1974; Lakshmanna, 1974; Singh, 1974; Nayer, 1975; Chatterjee, 1975; Mehta, 1976; Santhakumari, 1976; Maurya, 1976; Rastogi, 1976; Chitnis, 1977 and Ramanamma, 1978).

Some studies have revealed that the excessive involvement of children in domestic work is the main reason for the wastage in education. Their help is required in household work such as keeping watch over the house in the absence of adult members of the family and the compulsion to earn or to take a major share in domestic responsibility in order to release the adults for gainful work and the consequent attention to school work (Shah, 1972; Chatterjee, 1975; and Santhakumari, 1976).

Another set of studies reveals that employment is a reason for the wastage of education. Due to poverty; children get employment as unskilled labourers in factories or other organisation. Some children dropout due to seasonal employment. At the time of harvesting the crops, children being landless labourers, are engaged to cultivate the crops with the whole family (Soni, 1975; Chitnis, 1977 and Kirpal, 1978).

Occupational

Some studies have concluded that occupation of the parents lead to wastage in education. Scheduled Castes are the artisan classes and have their own parental occupations. They generally withdraw their children from school at early stage and engage the children in their own occupations (Shah, (1973; Singh, 1974).

Social

Some studies have pointed out that caste leads to wastage in education. In India, rural communities (the larger social setting) are not as complex and culturally diversified as urban communities. Rural community in India has still not lost its cultural stereotypes, thus there are villages which are conspicuous by their caste or occupational character. It is not uncommon to hear in this country—'This is a Brahmin 'village', This is an Ahir 'village'. It is not only in rural areas, but in urban areas also. This social disease compels children to drop-out from the schools (Sharma and Sapra, 1969).

Early marriage or betrothal significantly operates as a cause of westage in the case of girls. It is more pronounced at the primary and middle stage of education. It is found that children are withdrawn from school after betrothal or marriage particularly in the case of girls in the rural areas (Sapra 1967, Chauhan 1976). Another set of studies refers to the discriminating behaviour as a cause of wastage. The children of scheduled castes faced the difficulty of illtreatment in school particularly in urban areas. (Singh, 1974). It was also found that maltreatment and impolite attitude of teachers towards these children and their discrimination by teachers, general indifference and hostility towards the advance of Harijans on the part of upper caste, lead to wastage in education (Lakshmanna, 1974; Chatterjee, 1975; Maurya, 1976 and Yadav, 1984).

Social and family customs are also responsible for many cases of dropouts. Because of these, they believe in supersitions (Singh, 1974; Ramaswamy, 1974; Maurya, 1976). Chatterjee (1975) found that many of the parents regret the adverse affects that one dropout child from the family or neighbourhood have upon the others. Another important cause of wastage has been found to be the presence of first generation learners in schools. Most of the students are the first in their families to attend the school and as such parental help and encouragement are generally lacking for them in their effort to continue their education (Bose, 1969).

Conducive home environment is also important factor for the child's education. The Scheduled Castes homes particularly lack conductive environment for the study of their children as the facilities available to them for study are not sufficient. This leads to wastage in education (Singh, 1974; Lakshmanna, 1974; Mehta, 1976).

Educational

Stagnation is a major factor related to wastage and is warranted by the fact that the median period spent in class by dropouts is more then the time spent by stayins. The longer a child remains in one class, the more he is discouraged and probably neglected while his continued presence at school not only confess no benefit on him but also affects adversely the education of other pupils. Stagnation is due to a variety of factors, the main among which are the poor performance in studies, failures, poor quality of teachers, indifferent teaching, defective system of examination, load of syllabus and text books, lack of co-curricular activities and non-availability of textbooks, etc. (Chandrasekaraiah, 1969; Chaudhary, 1970; Lakshmanna, 1974; Nayer, 1975; Soni, 1975; Maurya, 1976; Santhakumari, 1976; Chitnis, 1977).

Faulty and defective system of admission also affects the education of the Scheduled Castes. In some schools, admission in grade I is kept open throughout the year where as in some schools the admissions are open only in the beginning of the session. As a result thereof those children who join the school towards the fag end of the academic session are treated as stagnation cases because they study only for few months and not for the whole years. Some schools have provision of entrance tests while others have not. There is no systematic procedure for the admission of these children in educational institutions (Naik, 1971). Educational status of the parents and family is no less important for the education of these people. Some studies have revealed that the presence of illiterate parents and larger number of illiterate members in the positively related to the phenomenon of wastage (Ramaswamy, 1974; Maurya, 1976; Shanthakumari, 1976 and Yadav, 1984).

Some studies have indicated that the lack of interest of the child as well as of his parents in education is a cause of wastage. Parents attitude is not very much encouraging motivating, and supportive towards education; and they have low aspiration level and frustating experience of the child at school (Singh, 1969; Shah, 1972; Naik, 1971; Dubey, 1974; Singh, 1974; Lakshmanna, 1974; Maurya, 1976; Misra, 1978; Ramanamma, 1978; Pimpley, 1978). Indequate facilities make children to dropout. Non-availability of educational aids like mid-day meals, books, states, uniforms etc., affect the education of scheduled caste children and lead to poor retention in schools (Chitnis, 1972; Dubey, 1974; Lakshmanna, 1974; Maurya, 1976; Yadav, 1979 and Yadav, 1983).

Some studies have revealed that delayed payment of scholarship is the main reason for the discontinuation of studies. Most of the times scholarships are distributed to the students at the end of the session and even after the session (Soni, 1975, Yadav, 1979 and Yadav, 1981).

Premi (1974) found that although there has been expension of elementary education and abolition of fees, yet the facilities are availed of more by "haves" than by deprived sections of socity whose children dropout at various stages.

However, besides social, economic, educational and occupational factors which lead to wastage in education, there are also certain other reasons which are responsible for discontinuation of education among scheduled castes. For instance, continuous illness of the pupils adversely affects their academic achievement and health which ultimately lead to wastage in education (Sapra, 1967; Mehta, 1976). Collection of money in the form of donation and irregular attendance have also been found to be the most important contributory factors responsible for the phenomenon of wastage in education (Lakshmanna, 1974). Distance of schools from the residence of teachers and also from the residence of the pupils has also been reported as the main reason for wastage in education (Chatterjee, 1975).

Tackling the Problem

The preceding section provided an overview of the reasons and causes of wastage in education. This section provides the guidelines for solving the complex problem of wastage in education.

Some situdies have pointed out that income level of the parents and family is the dominant factor in influencing the extent of retention in schools. So without eliminating these fundamental problems no satisfying of the problem is possible. Therefore, the parents should do extra work for increasing the income level of the family. (Shah, 1972; Nayer, 1975; Chatterjee, 1975).

Another set of studies suggested that special academic programmes and coaching classes should be organised for scheduled caste students for recovering their deficiencies in their subjects and in improving their academic performances. This will help in reducing the problem of wastage in education (Rastogi, 1976; Chitnis, 1977; and Yadav, 1984). Santha Kumari (1976) found that size of class and teacher-pupil relations also effect this problem. In primary and upper primary where there are 16 students or less, the rate of drop-out among scheduled caste children is less. In such a small size of group, the teacher can adopt a standard of teaching in accordance with their abilities which is suitable to them. This can be helpful in reducing the complex problem of wastage in education.

Pimply (1978) pointed out the awareness of reservation does have apositive relationaship with attendance. Those who are not aware are generally not attenders. The place or residence, however, does not seem to make any significant effect on school attendance. It has been realized that knowledge of facilities through personal experiences of a person may lead to school attendance. So the awareness of reservation of seats in educational institution should be created among scheduled castes so that this problem can be solved (Yadav, 1984). For tackling this problem, there should be provision of free supply of mid-day meals, biscuits, uniforms and other materials for the scheduled castes, so that they can be attracted and motivated towards the schools and remain in the schools (Yadav 1981). For the dropout students, programmes like non-formal education, partial education and adult education can be made, so that they can join schools, again after getting feedback from these agencies (Yadav, 1979).

4

Awareness of Scheduled Castes' About Educational Schemes

Awareness of scheduled castes about educational schemes has generally been considered the most important factor for their educational progress. In this chapter the various research studies conducted on awareness about educational schemes have been discussed in relation to demographic variables of age, sex, location and other variables like education, occupation and economic status of the scheduled castes which effect their awareness about educational schemes for their progress.

The studies in the area of awareness have covered a wide variety of variables pertaining to scheduled caste students and parents. Firstly, awareness has been studied in relation to students, parents and awareness within scheduled castes. Pimpley (1974), Singhi (1975), Dubey (1974), Nayer (1975), Valunjkar (1975), Gangrade (1974), Sachchidananda (1974), Chitnis (1974), George (1975), Shah (1974) and Yadav (1983) in their studies on educational problems of scheduled castes both at school and college levels found that most of the students were aware of the scholarship facilities, reservations in educational institutions and also aware of the constitutional provisions regarding the welfare of scheduled castes, whereas, Soni (1975), Rath (1974) and Rajagopalan (1974), Chauhan (1974) and Sachchidananda (1974) found that some of the school and college students are still not aware of the special reservation in educational institutions scholarship schemes and constitutional provisions for the welfare of scheduled castes. It will be of interest of know to what is the nature of the respondents who are unaware of these schemes.

Some studies have found a difference in the awareness of parents belonging to scheduled castes about educational schemes. Punalekar (1975), Santha Kumari (1975) and Premi (1974) found that the parents were aware of the educationa, concessions, financial concession, scholarships, stipends, freeships, reservation of seats for admission to educational institutions, coaching facilities provided and administered by Government/Harijan Welfare Department. However, Naik (1971), Vagiswari (1973), Maurya (1976), Yadav (1979), Nautiyal (1979) and Parvathamma (1973) found that the respondents were still unaware about the various facilities, aids, concessions in admission, special schemes and programmes provided by the government for the welfare of the scheduled castes, Taken together, the studies have presented a mixed bag of findings in this area.

Some studies indicate differential awareness within scheduled castes. Parmar (1978) on Mahayavanshi, a scheduled caste in Surat city found that the development of education in Mahayavanshi caste whows that among these there is an increasing awareness of the need for education which is further reflected in their increasing utilisation of educational facilities such as scholarship, freeships, and examination fees provided by the government. Abbasayulu (1977) and Yadev (1983) also found that the scheduled caste elite group was more aware about the educational schemes and benefits for their progress than all the scheduled castes taken together.

Another category of the studies refers to the area of awareness in relation to demographic variables of age and sex. The girl students were aware about the reservation for scheduled castes in government and public undertaking (Lal, 1974). But Pimpley (1974); Chitnis (1977) and George (1975) found that the awareness about reserved seats in educational institutions and facilities available for the welfare of scheduled caste, was more in boys than in girls.

Rastogi (1976) on the impact of Constitution provisions upon the uplift of scheduled castes found that the respondents of different age-groups are also aware of the different Constitutional provisions for protecting the interests of their communities. He further found that elder respondents are more aware of various legislative measures as compared to the yonger members.

Another set of studies refers to the area of awareness and the location of scheduled castes. Pimpley (1978) found that both the rural and urban attending children were equally aware and the place of residence does not seem to make any significant difference in their awareness. Rastogi (1976) and Yadav (1983) contradices this finding. He reports that all respondents drawn from urban areas are more aware of the constitutional provision regarding scheduled castes. Mukherjee (1975) corroborates this finding when he states that women belonging to scheduled castes are more aware about educational schemes in urban areas than in rural areas. Chitnis (1977) compared awareness of hostellers and non-hostellers. His study 'reveals' that hostellers have distinctly higher level of awareness than non-hostellers about schemes.

The awareness of scheduled caste children about educational schemes differ from district to district (Gangrade, 1974; Dubey, 1974). But Rajagopalan (1974), Soni (1975) and Rastogi (1976) found that the awareness of the respondents at the college stage belonging to corporation districts regarding educational schemes and reservation policies are higher as compared to other districts. So, the place of residence effects the awareness and utilisation of scheduled caste about educational schemes for their progress.

Other variables like social, educational, economic and occupational status of the scheduled caste respondents have also been studied in relation to their awareness of scheduled caste about educational schemes. Social restrictions create hinderance in the awareness of scheduled caste progress. The respondents are aware of the social restrictions on their admission to schools and colleges and feel the need for protective discriminations (Chitnis, 1977). The awareness of educational facilities increase the social status (Shantha Kumari. 1976). The welfare workers most must create an awareness about their rights and an atmosphere to assert them by reporting cases of infringement (Dubey, 1972).

Education is also found to be factor in increasing the awareness of scheduled caste about schemes for their progress. The awareness of schemes does have positive relationship with attenders and the lack of awareness was most pronounced in the case of non-attenders (Chauhan, 1967). Education in Mahayavanshi caste shows an awareness in the form of utilisation of educational schemes such as scholarships, freeships, and examination frees provided by the government (Parmar, 1978).

Malik (1971) and Malik (1979) found that greater percentage of educated respondents are aware of more important facilities, such as educational facilities, provisions of grants and less educated persons are comparatevely less aware of these facilities. Rastogi (1976) also found that the respondents doing their law graduation are comparatively more aware of various legislative measures than the respondents pursing other courses of study, quite a good number of respondents of all educational levels are aware of the various costitutional provisions.

Shantha Kumari (1976) on impact of welfare measures on the backward classes in Kerala found that the awareness transcends both the educational and occupational level of respondents and the awareness of educational facilities is an incentive for their children for jobs, which brings them a better job. This is an incentive for availing of existing educational facilities.

Economic status also increases the awareness of scheduled castes about educational schemes. The rise in income increases the awareness of the scheduled caste respondents about educational facilities (Shantha Kumari, 1976). The respondents in the large income brackets are comparatively more aware of various legislative measures as compared to their counterparts who are placed in lower income brackets (Rastogi, 1976). It can be the other way as well. They might be economically betters because of their higher awareness level.

In general, the research studies reviewed in this chapter highlight the extent of awareness and unawareness among scheduled castes about the reservation in educational and technical institutions, scholarships at various stages, educational schemes and programmes for their progress. Antecendent variables of awareness have also been discussed and presented in this research review.

5

Utilisation of Educational Schemes

The utilisation of educational schemes provided by the government for the welfare of the scheduled castes differs in different context. Only research studies can highlight the true picture of the utilisation of the educational schemes. This chapter reviews the various research studies conducted so far on utilisation of educational schemes and programmes and an attempt has made to present the findings of different studies pertaining to the utilisation of educational schemes in a systematic way.

The studies in the area of utilisation have covered a wide variety of variables pertaining to scheduled caste students and parents. Firstly the utilisation of schemes by the students and parents have been considered. Lal (1974), Adiseshiah (1975), Goyal (1974), Gangrade (1974), Pimpley (1974), Soni (1974), Dubey (1974), George (1975), Shah (1974), Parvathamma (1974), Chauhan (1975), Chitnis (1977), Desai (1974), Lakshmanna (1974), Sachchidananda (1974), Singh (1974) and Yadav (1983) found that most of the college and school students considered educational facilities, scholarships, stipends, freeships, reservation in admissions to educational institutions and various educational programmes to be useful, effectively utilised, beneficial for their educational progress and advancement. However, Rath (1974) and Chitnis (1974) found that the educational facilities are not adequate for the scheduled castes. But in most of the studies these facilities are considered to be useful for the progress of scheduled caste's education. The teachers as respondents also support the finding that scholarships and other schemes are very useful and fair in the promotion of education of scheduled castes (Nayer, 1975; Jha, 1973; Lakshmanna, 1974).

The scheduled castes differ in the use of educational facilities. It prepetuates the inadequacies within these people (Chauhan, 1976 and Yadav, 1983). The government assistance for education creates inequalities of utilisation between different groups within scheduled castes (Shah, 1974). The postmatric scholarship for being inequiteous in structuring and for fostering inequalities among Harijans, Chitnis (1977) and Premi (1977) observed the distinct caste and class pattern in use of educational facilities at higher stage.

Singh (1971) found that scholarship holders utilize a part of received amount on such items as buying books and other educational requirements, purchasing of clothes and on transports. Some spent less then Rs. 100 on hostel bills and examination fees, some spent more than Rs. 500 on above items. Some use a part of their scholarship for meeting family expenses. One obvious reason for this wrong utilisation of money was the poverty.

Yet another category of the studies refer to the area of utilisation in relation to demographic variables of age and sex. The male students considered these schemes more useful and satisfactory than the female students (Dubey, 1974 and Yadav, 1983), while Chitnis (1977) found that the scheduled caste women don't use these facilities as freely as scheduled caste men. Shah (1976) also found that male and female postmatric scholars indicate substantial difference in this aspect. More male postmatric scholar are coming for higher education than female postmatric scholars.

Some students showed the difference in the use of educational schemes in different age groups. Rastogi (1976) found that elder respondents are more aware and utilize the various legislative measures as compared to their younger counterparts.

Several studies facussed on the area of utilisation and the place of residence of the scheduled castes. Rastogi (1976) report that respondent coming from rural areas of U.P. show the maximum tendency of utilizing facilities provided by the government, while Shah (1976) found that the proporation of the scheduled caste scholars from urban areas in little less than double the proportion of their population residing in rural areas. The differential utilization of government assistance for higher education is related to the proportion of urban population among different scheduled castes. Dubey (1974) also found that more postmatric scholars were coming from the urban areas than rural areas. Ahmed (1973) found that differential utilisation of government assistance is not due to socio-economic reasons, but due to urban residence; the availability of educational facilities and the differences in various aspects of educational developments. The privileges benefit only some individuals. Premi (1974) found greater use of educational facilities offered by big cities and towns, whereas others have to content themselves with lower educational attainments.

The utilisation of educational schemes and government assistance differ from district to district. Surat district in Gujarat State was the highest in utilisation of government assistance for the higher education for the welfare of scheduled caste (Parmar, 1978; Shah and Patel, 1976). This may be due to the increasing involvement of voluntary organisations and due to the impact of Gandhi and his belief in constructive programmes.

Dubey (1974) found that highest respondents are from sibsagar district in Assam at college level, who think educational facilities are quite satisfactory, useful, and adequate; while Dubey (1974) at the school stage found that the highest number of scheduled caste respondents from

Lakhimpur and Dibrugarh feel that these facilities are not at all useful, adequate and satisfactory.

Hostels also affect the utilisation of schemes. Chinist (1977) found that college hostellers were dissatisfied with the facilities, while Trivedi (1977) found that the scholarships scheme was very useful for them. Dubey (1974) and Valunjkar (1975) also found that more hostellers felt that these educational facilities were useful, adequate and satisfactory then non-hostellers.

The utilisation of schemes does not differ in districts alone, but it differs from state to state. In every state certain scheduled caste communities within scheduled castes, which are in comparatively more advantageous circumstances to begin with, were able to get more benefits out of the schemes than other (Vyas, 1969; Chitnis, 1977; Parmar, 1978; Ram, 1976; Ramaswamy, 1974; Patwarahan, 1973; Premi, 1974; Shah, 1976; Chauhan, 1976; Das, 1971; and Hussain, 1972).

Other variables like social, educational, occupational and economic status of scheduled caste respondents have been studied in relation to their utilisation of schemes. Most of the respondents considered various educational programmes to be useful, effectively utilised, beneficial for their educational progress and social advancement (Rajagopalan, 1974; Gangrade, 1974; Pimply, 1974; Singhi, 1975; Singh, 1974; Sachchidananda, 1974; while Shah, 1974 found that scheduled castes have to face obstacles in the main stream of Indian social life due to these schemes. George (1975) also found that the system of separate hostels for scheduled caste students was considered socially unhealthy as it widened the gaps with higher caste students.

Parental education helps in utilising the schemes to the maximum. Shantha Kumari (1976), Rastogi (1976), Dubey (1974) and Gangrade (1974) found that father's education in the sense that the per cent of the students having favourable option on the usefulness of the educational facilities. Higher the education of the father, higher the utilisation of schemes by their children. George (1975) found that the parents needed to be educated about the government programme in order to properly utilise the resources. Empirical relationship was worked out between father's education and educational facilities.

Rastogi (1976) found that the incidence of utilisation is higher among the respondents, doing their graduation and after that doing their diploma/LLB Courses and least utilization is conspicuous in medical graduations. Malik (1971, 1979 and Yadav 1983) also found that higher the education of the respondents, the higher percentage of those who avail themselves of the opportunity, while Premi (1974) found that majority of respondents use educational facilities i.e. financial concessions such as freeships, stipends at high school and scholarship in college.

Most of the scheduled castes generally engage in low level of occupations. More occupations increased their utilisation of educational schemes. Most of the postmatric scholars were found from the white collar occupations (Shah, 1976).

The differential utilisation of government assistance is due to socio-economic reasons. Pathsudu (1971), Pimpley (1976), Goyal (1974), Yadav (1980), Premi (1977) and Saxena (1968) found that greater advantages of the programmes are availed by the people from hign socio-economic group, advanced sections and privileged families from scheduled castes. The postmatric scholarship, the central piller of all educational facilities at higher stage, tends to favour the 'haves, rather than 'have not's' or depriveds sections. Dogra (1977) found that low socio-economic status of Harijans has resulted in a massive under utilisation of facilities.

Gangrade (1974) found that all the students belonging to the comfortable and average economic position found the educational facilities useful. The students who were of the opinion that facilities are not proving useful had poor economic condition, while Lal (1974) found poor economic status students hold the view that educational facilities are quite useful.

The awareness of constitutional provision increases the utilisation rate of schemes. Rastogi (1976) found that all those who are aware of constitutional provisions have also availed of the benefit provided under the act with regard to other legislative measures. Mailik (1971), Malik (1979) found that educated respondents have greater knowledge of the facilities provided and avail these to a greater extent than the less educated persons.

Aggarwal (1976) found that most of the people list educational scholarships as the more useful privilage then any other. This corresponds closely to high level of awareness of privilage among the respondents. Not only did a large number know this but they list it as the first item when asked to identify the various privilages. Parmar (1978) also found that there is an increasing awareness of the need for education in Mahayavanshi caste which is further reflected in their increasing utilisation of educational facilities such as scholarships, freeships and examination fees and other facilities by the government.

Premi (1974) found that greater awareness of freeships, stipends and scholarships, suggests that these facilities are universally available and widely used. Lesser awareness of other financial facilities suggests that either these particular facilities have not been properly published or they have not been introduced at many places; while Pimpley (1974) found that they are aware of the facilities provided to them, but in general, a large number of educable age group had not availed of these facilities.

Some studies discovered the factors for utilising the schemes effectively. Misra (1978) found that the utilisation and non-utilisation depend on several factors such as family background, attitude of the community members, attitude of non-scheduled caste members, teachers role and attitude of the members of the family toward education, social status of family, and lack of conducive environment. Shanta Kumari (1976) also found that the above mentioned factors affect the utilisation of educational facilities.

This chapter highlighted the utilisation of educational benefits/schemes by the scheduled castes. It also reflected the determinants and antecedents of utilisation of educational schemes in tems of sex and place of living with respect to their social, educational, economic and occupational status after analysing the researches conducted in this field.

6

Constraints Utilisation on the Educational Schemes

The scheduled castes have been facing lot of problems and difficulties in availing the different facilities and benefits provided by the government for improving their educational status. Here an attempt has been made to review such research studies conducted so far in this area for reflecting the various constraints and difficulties which generally come in their way in availing these facilities.

Proper publicity of the educational schemes creates awareness among the scheduled castes. Soni (1975) found that proper communication of government policies in small and rural areas is found somewhat lacking in effectiveness. Nautiyal (1979) and Yadav (1983) also found that there is not enough publicity regarding the exact nature of concessions facilities permissible to scheduled castes. The role of mass media is significant in publicising the educational schemes. In a few research studies it was found that those who are illiterates have less exposure to mass media, particularly the news paper and fail to get benefits from the schemes. Those who are literate and educated have more exposure to mass media and avail of maximum benefits from the schemes (Parvathamma, 1974; Gangrade, 1974: Goyal, 1974; Chitnis, 1977; Pimpley, 1974: Sachchidananda,

1974; Valunjakar 1975 and Yadav, 1983). Educated biased way of publicity of educational schemes has creased a privileged class among the scheduled castes, and usually, the privileged comes from better off families. This, in turn, leads to intra-scheduled castes inequalities. (Chitnis, 1975 ; Khurana, 1980; sharma, 1974). The help tends to benefit the 'haves' rather deprived section of the society (Premi, 1977). Several low levels of occupational categories (i.e. sweepers, vendors, tanners are not represented among the scheduled caste postmatric scholars (Shah, 1976). So due to inadequate publicity of educational schemes a number of needy students fail to avail of such educational opportunities.

The problem of publicity is followed by the cumbersome procedural difficulty. The scheduled castes face difficulties in securing forms, comprehending the language of the forms, getting scheduled caste certificate, attestation from M.P./ Gaxetted Officer, and submitting application forms. (Dubey 1974). Gangrade, (1974) also found, both at school and college stage that the formal procedure to obtain facilities, consumes a lot of their time. George (1975) found that most of the parents belonging to scheduled castes, face difficulty at the time of taking stipend of their children. The parents reported that the system of distribution of stipend is complicated. This cumbersome procedure effects a large population of the scheduled caste and deprive them from the benefits.

Conditions of eligibility present another road block in the way of education of scheduled castes. Many students reported that failure in the examination was the main reason for the discontinuation of their studies. The failure in the examination means loss of scholarships and stipend. The student fail not because of their indifference but becasue of cultural deprivation and biased examination. With out these educational benefits the scheduled caste students can not afford to complete their studies on their own and they are virtual drop-outs (Chauhan, 1975 and Yadav, 1983).

Shah (1976) also reports, that means test being applied by the government for the postmatric scholars succeeds more or less in restricting the award of postmatric scholarship to the children of the scheduled caste who are generally employed in low level occupatiors. Thus, the conditions of eligibility are biased towards the advantages one in this disadvatageed group, while the deserving are left out.

Due to these incentives for their education, most of the scheduled caste students and parents face difficulty to discriminatory behaviour, prejudices and fear complexes ariring from their experience with those who administer the schemes. Chandersekharaih (1969) found the discriminatory treatment of scheduled caste children in privates schools. Instances of ill-treatment are often reported in hostels for Harijans run by the government or private management (Pankaj, 1977). Six students from Gujarat complained that they were insulted when they went to collect their scholership as the clerical staff called them the 'Son-in-law' of the government. Four of them informed that the teacher did not hesitate to insult them before others and made it clear that they were considered as 'drag on the community' (Karlekar, 1975).

The beneficiaries from these programmes earn for discrimination behaviour, caste hatrted, non-cooperation, humiliation and supperession from higher castes. (Goyal, 1974). Due to this discriminat ory behaviour some students feel that the schemes for the facilitation of education of the scheduled caste provided by the government damage the self respect of the community. Scheduled caste people become dependent on the programmes and their initiative is killed, (Singh, 1974; Debey, 1973; Lal, 1974). Ramaswamy (1974) and Chitnis (1974) also found that the provision of scholarship, reservation of seats in educational institutions and legislatures and special allocation of funds for the welfare of scheduled caste have served to reinforce the separate identify of these castes rather than integrate them with the rest of the society, had a very poor opinion. Such fear complex hampers the progress of the scheduled castes.

Effective administration and implementation of the programmes for the welfare of the scheduled caste is likely to leae to the progress of their education. But prevalent chronic delays, currupt practices and misappropriation of dunds present hurdles of insurmountable magnitude. Most of the scheduled caste students and parents report the prevalence of the delay in the award of scholarship which create lot of inconveneience to these people. Sometimes they get money after they leave the school/college. (Jha, 1973; Parvathamma, 1974; Dubey, 1974), Commissioner of scheduled castes and Tribes (1969-70). Administrative delays cause irregul arities in the reimbursement of scholarships. There fore, sometime scholarships are given in lumpsum which is commonly spent for meeting the other domestic requirements rather than the purpose for which it is meant (Patwardhan, 1973), Commissioner of scheduled caste and Tribes, (1968-69). The pattern of social welfare administration, present of very discouraging and dismal picture today. The administrative agencies do not have adequate and competent staff. They are not satisfied with the administration of the programmes. The absence of healthy relationship between scheduled caste students and those who administer programmes present barrier to their utilisation (Sharma, 1976; Lal, 1975; Pimpely, 1978; Goyal, 1974; Rajagopalan, 1974; Gangrade, 1974; Singh, 1974; Soni, 1975; George, 1975; Lakshamanna, 1974; Valunjkar, 1975: Chitnis, 1977; Premi, 1979).

Malik (1979) criticised the working of the government machinery as such on the ground that the heads of the departments and leaders are from the non-scheduled castes. Dubey (1973) and Aggrawal (1973) also found that most of the respondents complained that it wasteg of mony, time and effort even to apply for any privileges, if they did not have the plitical influence. The allocation of funds is faulty.

Besides, Aggrawal (1976) and Pankaj (1977) reported that the official are found engaged in corrupt practices and mis-appropriation of funds. For example, government are providing funds for the construction of the hostels, but the funds are mis-appropriated and fictitious figures are fed. When any inspector or high official visits the hostels, Harijans boys are brought from outside for the purpose of showing the numbers, they are given a day's food and lodging with some money and are sent away as soon as the inspectors back is turnd. Lakshmanna (1974) found that during 1973-74 bogus hostels had drawn Rs. 5.87 lakhs in one district alone. This was a clear proof of the prevalent corruption and lack of supervision by the government authorities. Malik (1979) found that every thing is done on paper by the government and nothing is practised in reality. Azad (1976), Rajagopalan (1974), Singh (1974) and Desai (1974) found that general economic position of scheduled castes is so poor that inspite of scholarships they are unable to pursue higher education while (Soni, 1975; Chitnis, 1976; Rastogi, 1976 and Parvathamma, 1974) found that except scholarship they have to depend on their parents. Premi (1974) found that at elementary school stage it could be possible to study without financial support but she found it is difficult to continue higher education without financial support. Financial concessions are important motivating forces by the respondents.

The corrupt practices in administration and mis-apprppriation of funds is accompanied by the inadequacy of educational facilities. Most of the students and parents belonging to scheduled caste report that the existing amount of schemes and scholarships are grossly inadequate. With this amount of scholarship they find it difficult even to meet the cost of note-books (Goyal, 1974; Rajagopalan, 1974; Sharma, 1976; Gangrade, 1974; Pimpley, 1974; Singh, 1975; Desai, 1975; Parvathamma, 1974; Rath, 1974; Chitnis, 1977; Trivedi, 1977; Singh, 1975).

Most of the students offered Arts subjects due to absence of facilities because science students have to incur more expenditure on laboratory dress and on technical instruments. (Sachchidananda 1974). This finding is supported by the report (1971-72, 72-73) of the commissioner for scheduled castes and scheduled Tribes. In west Bengal it was found the exemption from payment of tuition fees is not granted to all the scheduled caste students, but only to 41 communities. This causes hardships to many deserving students from the remaining castes.

The scheduled caste students also faces difficulties in getting accommodation in the hostels (Lal, 1975; Rajagopalan, 1975; Gangrade, 1975; Soni, 1975; Dubey, 1974; Shah, 1974; Lakshmanna, 1974; Valunjkar, 1975; Vyas, 1969; Trivedi, 1977; Rastogi, 1976 and Premi, 1974) found that the existing number of hostels are not sufficient. Hostel accomodation and facilities provided for them are unsatisfactory and inadequate. Vyas (1969) and Rastogi (1976) further said that all the respondents residing in the hostels run by the central and state governmentt are not receiving the facilities of free lodging, medical and recreational facilities. In addition, even the available facilities are not up to the mark. Dubey (1974) also reported the unsatisfactory conditions of these hostels. They are not only badly managed, but even the prescribed accommodation requirements are not met. They were found to be overcrowded, unhygenie, and the food was inadequate both in the quality as well as quantity.

Most of the students face many difficulties in getting admission to various courses against reserved seats, (Gangrade, 1974). Dubey (1974) found that they did not get admission in Assam Medical College, though there were reserved seats. Frequent refusal to admission in private schools for the scheduled caste children was commonly observed (Chandersekaraih, 1969).

By way of conclusion, the government has launched a number of educational schemes for the progress of education of the scheduled castes, but the implementation of schemes present a number of problem for the beneficiaries. The problem of inadequate publicity, cumbersome administrative procedure, indifferent implementation machinary, corrpupt practices, inadequate hostel facilities, difficulties in admission to educational institutions, delay in disbursement of amount are the some of significant ones.

7

Facilitators for Implementation of Educational Schemes

The government of India has provided several constitutional measures and safeguards for the scheduled castes. When these safeguards are implemented, then a number of problem arises. So far finding out the solutions complex problems and difficulties, various research studies have been conducted. Here the review of such research studies have been made to highlight the various solutions and answers of the constrainst which generally come at the time of transcation of the various schemes.

The first problem posed by the respondents refer to the inadequacy of publicity. In order to make publicity effective, suitable media need to be used. Lakshamanna (1975) wants the social workere to be pressed into service for the purpose in addition to the printed materials. Special programmes should be launched through mass-media (Rastogi, 1979). A survey should be conducted to indentify rural areas and urban localties having a large scheduled caste population for assessing their needs for the educational facilities and take immediate step to provide them the inputs if they are willing to avail in case are not making their use due to poverty. This will help in providing the bublicity in a wider base and will help increase awareness of scheduled caste students about the schemes.

The problems of publicity is followed by the cumber some procedure of submitting application for availing the schemes. To make the procedure functional, several steps have been suggested. The respondents wanted the application forms printed. These should be in regional languages. The documents may be accepted even afterward, since sometimes it is difficult to obtain these particularly, when the date of submission is very close. Conditions of availability should be suitably modified to enhance their utilisation by a wider population. This will help the scheduled caste students to avil the maximum benefits from these schemes (Rastogi, 1976).

As pointed out in the preceding section, discriminatory behaviours, prejudicial attitude and fear complex among the scheduled castes poses a serious problem in utilising educational schemes. In order to overcome this problem proper guidence is needed to protect the scheduled caste students from infreiority complex through councelling. The students needed to be educated about the existing facilities and their purpose (George, 1975). The scholarships awarded to the students should be sent to their parents directly. This will avoid the possible discrimination among the students in the school (Chauhan, 1975). The reservation of seats in educational institutions should be increased. Encouragement of freeinter-caste dining, marriage, children education upto 14 years, improvement in the economic status should be emphasised (Rastogi, 1976). Children of scheduled caste elites should not be given such facilities. Instead, these facilities should be extended only to those who are really needy (Sharma, 1974). Gupta (1976) also suggested the solution for overcoming this problem. He suggested that the theory of 'Social work practice' should be such that the profession can lean upon it. One has to create an awareness in the minds of the clientale about the problems they face and at the same time, to make the clientale aware of the resources they own both as individual as well as in collectives situations to solves the problem. This will help in reducing the prejudical attitude of higher castes.

The problem of delay in the scholarships, corrupt practices in the administration, and misappropriation of funds are quite common these days. For overcoming these the delay in the award of scholarships, Singh, 1974; Jha, 1973; Dubey, 1974; and commissioner for scheduled caste and Scheduled Tribe (1971-72, 1972-73) suggests that the scholarships should be awarded within a month of the submission of application. Further the scholarships should be paid to him before he is required to pay his fees or spend on maintenance and after he has got into debt (pisharody, 1972). A separate cell may be set up in the Directorate of Public Instruction for the disbursement of scholarships and for maintaining an upto date record (Jha, 1973; Singh, 1974). To avoid the mis-apropriation of the funds. the teachers suggested periodic checking from the records as well as from the students. Some think that the scholarships awarded to the student should be sent to their parents. This will check the misuse of the money by the students (Chauhan, 1975). A review should be made to see that schemes benefit more the backward amongst these communities or not (Khurana, 1981; Yadav, 1979).

Most of the scheduled caste parents and students complained against the administration and implementation of the educational schemes. In some studies suggestions are made to remove the administrative difficulties. The problem of social welfare administration have got to be viewed with serious concern (Sharma, 1976; Chauhan, 1975). Corruption should be eliminated properly. Awareness of reservation facilities by the scheduled caste students is an essential factor for implementation of such programmes (Singh, 1974).

Programmes should be revised and properly implemented. The placement of persons for administering these schemes should be either from the scheduled caste themselves or if they are to be from the other communities it may be insured that only those who have sysmpathetic attitude towards these castes are allocated work in this respect (Dubey, 1974). Unless government brings forward a law which fixes responsibility for administrative lapses and provide for punishment of those officer who fail to implement the constitution safeguards, these safeguards will continue to be floated with inpunity (Ramdhan, 1978). From the experience so far in the planning and emplementation of various schemes it has been gathered that welfare programmes should be conducted and implemented through voluntary organisations particularly because the worker will be from the strata of the society to which the problem and programme pertain (Sahai, 1978).

Other studies also suggested solution for this problem. Acharya (1971) found that the work should be entrusted only to such officers who have been exhibited a real sense of service to the cause of the backward community. Merely mechanical utilisation of funds alloted for the welfare of the scheduled caste will ever solve this vast problem. It should be ensured by all means that the funds alloted are utilised on schemes, drawn up with thought and imagination, so as to achieve the desired effect within the shortest possible time.

There is lack of coordination amongst the various administrative agencies. For formal action and implementation of programmes, high level coordination committee should be set up at the headquarters and the districts levels. Monitoring arrangements should be made with the coordinating function resting with education department. Monitoring of programmes may be highlighted in a chapter in the administrative reports of the education department for reviewing the educational progress of the scheduled castes annually. At the centre also there should be an institution which may be assigned monitoring of the progress of education of these communities by undertaking evaluation studies at the national level (Premi, 1979).

The problem of administration and implementation of scheme is followed by the inadequate amount of scholarships. Khurana (1980) and Yadav (1979) suggest that the rate of scholarships and distribution of concessions will have to be revised and the amount of scholarships should be sufficient to meet the cost of their education.

Inadequate hostel accomodation is also quite conspicuous. Several suggestions have been put forth to overcome this problem. (Singh, 1974) and commissioner for scheduled castes and Scheduled Tribes (1971-72, 1972-73) suggested that hostel facilities for both boys and girls need to be improved particularly for the latter. Dubey (1973) also recommended opening of "Model government hostel", training of the wardens, matrons, taking over the subsidised hostel by the government, and auditing of the accouts in order to prevent misappropriation of funds. SCERT Tamil Nadu (1974-76) recommended that there is need to improve the percentage of residential scholarships so that they may stay in special hostel with better facilities for study. Pimpley (1975) suggested that women hostels should be attached with every women's and co-educational college where sufficient seats should be reserved for the scheduled caste students. This will help in tackling the hostel problem of scheduled caste students.

The problem of admission in various educational institutions against reservation seats is faced by the scheduled castes. In order to overcome this problem, Pimpley (1975) suggest that sufficient seats should be reserved for scheduled caste students invarious type of educational institutions, so that they can avail the benefits easily for their educational progress. Rastogi (1976) suggested that the sympathetic attitude toward these people can help in tackling this ticklish problem.

The adove studies have suggested to tackle the various problems faced by the scheduled caste in the utilisation of educational schemes for their progress.

8

Motivational Tendencies, Intelligence, Academic Achievement and Adjustment Among Scheduled Castes

It is a common feeling among the people that scheduled castes are inferior in academic achievement, less motivated, least adjustment and less intelligent as compared to other castes. But the above statement has no basis and generalisation about some fact or matter can't be made without the availability of lage number research studies. No doubt some researches have been conducted in this area and have shown a mixed findings. An attempt has been made in this chapter to review all the psychological studies on scheduled caste conducted so far in this area and presented them in a systematic order so that some conclusions can be drawn on the basis of the findings of these researches.

1. Motivational Tendencies

Motivational tendencies are the most important for the development of the child's personality. The studies conducted on motivational tendencies so far have been reviewed in this section. The available studies have been classified under achievement motivation, fear, anxiety, aggression and learning task etc.

Achievement Motivation

The result of the most of the research studies about the achievement motivation of backward classes particularly Negros abroad and scheduled castes and scheduled tribes in India are not unanimous. In same cases (Bradburn, 1963; Cameron, 1965; Poussaint Alvin, 1968; Himes, 1973; Minigione, 1965 and Mossback, 1969), the coloured population have been found inferior in achievement motivation. But in some other studies no such discrimination was found (Barial, 1966; Hall, 1975; Mehta, 1967; and Minigone, 1968). In few other cross cultural studies of white and coloured, South African Adolescents, only certain minority group who were subjected to discrimination, were found having low achievement motivation (Lazarus Kessel and Botha 1969). Some other studies had showed that socially backward classes have higher n—achievement motivation than socially upper classes (Gokulnathan, 1972). But in this case, the study was on students who migrated from a village to some urban areas and were studying in some urban based schools.

Anxiety

Julka (1963) and Choksi (1975) conducted the study on anxiety. Julka compared Bhills and non-Bhills on anxiety and found that two groups did not differ in their anxiety level in any significant level. In the study of Amita Chokri also, no difference could be found in the anxiety level of persons from different socio-economic background. In the studies of Joshi (1980) and Singh (1982), majority of the scheduled caste students suffered from fear complex, anxiety and lack of confidence and they were more worried and had anxiety towards examination and scholarship. They had positive attitude towards schools and mothers but had negative attitude towards society, elite group and the opposite sex. But Usharri (1978) found that the disadvantaged pupils were less keenly interested in their academic pursuits and had poor personal efficiency in the planning and use of their term due to anxiety and depression. Laxmidevi (1980) reported that the major problems of the harijan children as perceived by the teachers were inferiority feeling. As regards fear motivation, Kamlesh (1981) reported that the mean scores of the urban non-scheduled caste was above average and it was below in case of scheduled castes.

Aggression

In the study of Julka (1963), it was found that non Bhills producing significantly more themes of aggression then Bhill children. Poussaint Alvin Etal (1968) also found impeded aggression in the Negroes. Modsen (1967) in his study on cooperative and competative motivation found that the middle class boys from urban areas were more cooperative than urban low and rural middle class ones. Besides, Parkash (1981) indicated factors namely assertive and self crital domination attitude, low integeration, negativism and apprehensiveness preference for one's own decision obstructiveness and aggressiveness, escapasim attitude and self opinion for the caste Hindu group, for the scheduled caste group the factors were assertion and collective action, practicalness and not free from obstacles, free from inhibition and participation, independent and self confidence attention, getting behaviours and lack of self criticism, demoralised emotion and action, accompalishment and developing collectives.

Academic Motivation

In this area Amita Choksi (1975) conducted a study in five english medium schools of Baroda and could not find any significant differences among students coming from various socio-economic status. Elearnor R. Hall (1975) also observed that racial differences in academic achievement may not hold true for particular sub-groups. However, Cameron (1965) found middle class students better than working class and Canadian Indians on learning task under non-material rewards. Similarly Mishra (1968) and Chitra (1969) found culture background playing a significant role in the determination of learning. Katz (1967) also found achievement gap existing among white and Negroes students. In addition to above, Bose (1969) narrated that unattaracted school environment and school curriculum lead to warning of the interests of the child in the school. Besides, overcrowding non-availability of right type of teachers and faulty supervision were found the reasons which did not motivate the students to learn in a effective manner.

Fear Motivation

Julka (1963) in his study on Bhills and non-Bhills did not find significant difference in these two groups in their fear motivation but Singh (1982) found significant difference between scheduled caste and non-scheduled caste students in fear motivation.

2. Intellegence

Many research studies have been conducted to find the significance of intelligence between scheduled castes and non-scheduled castes. The findings of these studies are not uniform and common. Das, (1969); Singh, (1974); Gangrade, (1974); Karlekar, (1975); Singh (1975) and Nayer (1975) conducted the studies on teachers to investigate the intellectual level between scheduled caste and non-scheduled caste students. In studies showed that scheduled caste students were much poorer in calibre and intelligence than the other students belonging to higher castes. The teachers perceived that the scheduled caste students had lower level of intellectual capacity than the other castes. Besides these, some studies were conducted on the students. Aggarwal, (1975); Thakural, (1977); Singh, (1981); Rath, (1979); Parkash; (1981) and Gaur (1987) found the significance difference between scheduled castes and non-scheduled castes in the mean intelligence scores. The non-scheduled caste students were found more intelligent on the average than the scheduled caste students. It was stated further that the level of intelligence was affected by the places of their livings. The rural non-scheduled caste groups showed significantly higher verbal intelligence than scheduled caste group. The same significant difference was found on intelligence in urban areas between the two groups (Gaur, 1987). The sex differences were also noticed on the scores of intelligence between the two groups. The male students scored higher on intelligence than female students (Rangari, 1981). Besides this, Parkash (1981) reported same factors responsible for the intellectual level. He said that the students belonging to scheduled castes whose parents had better houses, better education and from higher income group scored higher score on intelligence than those scheduled caste parents who belong to lower income group and uneducated families.

Some studies like Barial (1966), Ushasri (1978) and Sutradhar (1982) did not find any significant difference in the intelligence level of the students belonging to different social classes. However, Shanthamani (1970) found that caste has an influence on intelligence of students. Singh (1978) also emphasised that scheduled castes are deprived class in our society. They have to face various social and financial problems and due to these handicaps they have almost no opportunity to develop their intellectual capacities and abilities. Besides, the scheduled castes are far away from scientific development and the gradual changes occuring as a result of industrialization or modernization which play a greater role in sustaining their orthodoxy and conservative feelings. Their orthodoxy manifests more in the rearing of their children. No doubt orthodox parents find themselves unable to develop their children's knowledge, intellectual level and raise them in a proper way.

3. Academic Achievement

In the studies of academic achievement of Lal (1975), Lakshmanna (1975), Valunjkar (1975) and Nayer (1975), most of teachers reported that scheduled caste students were poor in studies in comparison to non-scheduled caste students. They also pointed out some reasons like poor in intelligence, poor comprehension, uncongenial home environment and poverty etc., which are responsible for their poor academic achievement. They had suggested that the teachers should pay more attention towards these children and reservation Policy can also be useful for them for their academic achievement.

Some studies were conducted on the school students also. The findings of these studies were similar to the teachers studies. Higher caste students achieve significantly higher than the scheduled caste students (Singh. 1975; Sharma, 1975; Kumar & Murlidharan, 1978; Suri, 1979; Ameerjan, 1979; and Aikara, 1980). The other studies like Sharma (1982), Vastisri, (1978); Sutradhar, (1982); Khobragade, (1981) and Laxmidevi (1980) reported that the percentage of retention was highest in class X and the percentage of detention was highest in class I. Dantawala (1976) and Suri (1979) expressed the five main characteristics of educational backwardness. These were (1) poor enrolment in terms of numbers at different stages of the educational system (2) consistantly poor performance (3) heavy rate of drop-out (4) clustering in inferrior and less prestigious institutions (5) inability of students from the weaker sections to enter professional and technical courses. Shivashan Kara (1981) reported that the intelligence, personality adjustment and school adjustment variables were responsibles for their poor performance but Nagaraju (1977) in his study found that the average achievement of the scheduled caste students was same as that of the general group.

Anotner set of studies were conducted on the college students. The researchers faund the same result as in the case of school students. The mean academic achievement index was found higher in non-scheduled caste College students than the scheduled caste students (Gupta, 1979; Bindu, 1974 and Barkar, 1982). The difference between scheduled caste and non-scheduled caste students in academic achievement was also noticed in engineering and professional colleges. It was due to the past academic background (I.I.P., 1982). But

Adiseshiah and Ramanathan (1979) reported that the percentage of scheduled caste literarcy had increased from 14.66 per cent in 1966 to 26.00 per cent in 1971 showing an increase in the annual ratio at 1.26 per cent over 0.8 per cent for non-scheduled castes. Chitnis (1975) reported that inferiority of scheduled caste students was even more pronounced with respect to performance at college level. The percentage of enrolment in engineering and medical college was very much small.

The scheduled caste students opt for easy subjects in higher education as compared to other caste students. Most of the students from scheduled caste generally offered the art subjects in higher education which the students from other castes generally offered the science subjects (Sachchidananda, 1975 and Adiseshiah 1979). In the study of Rao (1976), overwhelming enrolment of scheduled castes students was found in bachelor of arts courses. It was also revealed that they were very poor in qualifying the examination. The enrolment in bachelor in science courses was from the higher castes. Singh (1982) reported that three commulative records cards of the students over a three years periods indicated an improvement in performance. Sixty four per cent of these students had been an residentials school for over three years. The majority of the students had academic problems like poor handwriting, difficulties in english and mathematics subjects; lack of books and food etc. They suffered from uncertainity about future, inferiority and indcision particularly in regards to vocations and higher education. But Nagaraju (1977) reported in his study that the achievement in science and mathematics among scheduled castes students staying in hostels was the same as that of the day scholar of the higher caste.

A few other studies have pointed out that academic acheivement vary within the scheduled castes have better academic performance than the total population. Das (1968) stated that some sub-castes within scheduled castes like Kanwar and Sansi have crossed over the line of achievement of the tolal population in respect of literarcy at primary and junior basis educational level. Singh (1986) also expressed the variation of academic performance within scheduled castes. He found that in academie achievement, the respondents belonging to four castes Qusadh, Chamar, Dhobi and Passi did better than other scheduled castes. Dom and Mehar also leave behind other castes. Here three cluster were formed. Cluster one consisted of Dushad, Chamar, Dhobi and Passi. Cluster two consisted of Dom and Mehar. Cluster three consisted to other castes. The castes in cluster one were different from other castes so far as their desire to achieve more is concerned. These castes respondents seem to be set for achieveing higher and higher. This showed better academic culture developed among these castes.

Academic achievement differed sexwise also. Sachchidananda (1974) and Aggarwal (1982) conducted a study on girls of both the communities and found that scheduled caste girls were poor in academic achievement than non-scheduled caste girls. Sharma (1975) investigated that both male and female children were found inferior in academic achievement than high caste group. Singh (1969) reported that upper caste people have almost 100 per cent literacy whereas in the scheduled castes, 50 per cent males were literate. It was also marked between males and females (Chitnis, 1975) and scheduled caste women did better than men (Rangari, 1981). The place of living has also an impact on the performance and academic achievement of the children. Chitnis (1975) conducted an intensive analysis of scheduled castes literacy in Maharashtra and indicated the disparity between the scheduled castes and the rest of the population in the district having largest scheduled castes population. It was more marked in urban areas than in rural areas.

Economic factor plays a crucial role for the improvement of the academic achievement. Some studies have conducted on this aspect and found that economic factor was the reason for the lower academic achievement among the scheduled caste students (Sharma 1975, and Singh 1982). In the Bombay study, Chitnis (1975) provided several indicators to prove that the academic performance of scheduled caste students does not compare favourably with that of their non-scheduled caste students due to not equal income or occupational differences in their background. Harijan, poor and rich were found to be backward in word reading and speech. The brahmin children even when comparable economic level did better than Harijan in short term recall. The harijan students committed a large number of errors in writing auditory material and the harijans children were found to have less relatively, less facility with cross model coding than with unimodel coding although this they shared with poor brahmin children. Besides this education and occupation of the partners had influence on the academic achievement of their children. This holds true in occupational status also.

4. Adjustment

In the study of Singh (1982) found that majority of the scheduled caste students were well adjusted with the non-scheduled caste students. Choksi (1975) also conducted the study in this area and found that the students from different social background did not find significant differences. But Sharma (1979), Rangari (1981), Sharma (1982), and Sen (1982) found significant difference on adjustment between scheduled castes and non-scheduled castes students. Rangari reported that there was significant difference between scheduled caste non-scheduled caste students on the sub-variables of adjustment also. By and large the non-scheduled caste students showed better adjustment in different mean scores then the scheduled caste students. Sen (1982) said that negative adjustment was very high in scheduled caste students. Ushasri reported that the socially disadvantaged and the socially non-disadvantaged group significantly differed with regard to academic adjustment scores. Sharma found that the adjustment of scheduled castes and backward students was very much unsatisfactory as against the condition of general upper class students which was reported as satisfactory.

In some other studies, the adjustability of the students of both the communities have been studied with regard to their place of livings and their sex. Kamlesh (1981) found that the level of adjustment among the urban scheduled caste students was lower as compared to rural scheduled caste students whereas the non-scheduled caste students both in rural and urban areas did not have adjustment problems. These findings were supported by Sharma (1979) and Rangari (1981).

The sex had significant impact on adjustment. The females had higher adjustment scores than males and also the females had more psychological problems and comlexes than the males (Sharma, 1979). The same findings was found in the study of Rangari (1981). Besides this, Sharma (1979) reported some other significant differences on adjustment between scheduled castes and backward classes students in comparison to general students. It was reported that the adjustment of both the comparable groups in 1977 indicated that the adjustment of the scheduled caste and backward class students had considerably improved. The faculty differences did not affect the adjustment scores and the levels of education. The socio-economic status had no effect on adjustment but Kamlesh (1981) reported that the socio-economic had impact on adjustment and emphasised that the level of adjustment among the scheduled caste belonging to lower socio-economic status was below normal.

There are some other factors which influence the adjustment of the scheduled caste students in home and the school. Aggarwal (1970) found some of the adjustment problems and correlations with some factors in his study. He said that adjustment problems in home, school and social areas decrease themselves with increase of the age of the children but it increases in case of health and emotional areas. It was also found that teacher perception of pupil adjustment is by and large in agreement with that of the parents. Shivashankara (1981) also conducted that study on factors which influence adjustment of scheduled caste students with the higher caste students. He reported that the variables which influence the socially disadvantaged including the scheduled caste students were intelligence, personality adjustment and school adjustment.

The preceding discussion has focussed the motivational tendencies, intelligence, academic achievement and adjustment problems of scheduled castes in relation to non-scheduled caste including their different dimensions. These psychological factors have made clear that scheduled caste people require attentions for improving their status by the government. It will have to make great efforts to bring the scheduled caste people at per with general caste people.

9

Attitude, Self-concept and Aspiration Level Among Scheduled Caste

The psychological factors like attitude, self-concept and aspiration level play vital role in the development of the personality. If one has positive attitude, high self-concept and aspiration level, the difficult task also becomes very easy and can achive the desired objectives in specified time and if one has negative attitude, low self-concept and aspiration level, the easier things also become very difficult task. In this chapter an attempt has been made to review the available researches conducted so far in these areas in a systematic order so that some inferences can be drawn for the development of scheduled caste people.

Attitude

Attitude is one of the most important psychological factors which affect the progress of the scheduled caste people, Some studies have been conducted on teacher's attitude towards scheduled caste students. The result of these studies do not show clear cut direction but showed mix findings. Singh (1982) reported that the teachers had a feelings of partiality and biased attitude towards these students. Joshi (1980) also supported the above findings and found that the students perception about their teachers was not favourable and indicated that the teachers had not been able to present the right image of themselves. Majority of the teachers working in backward classes belonging to upper classes had their prejudices towards scheduled caste students. As a result of prejudices, the teachers suggested only lower level of occupation for scheduled caste students. But Pathak (1981) put up different view and found that majority of the students expressed positive attitude towards their teachers. Sachchidananda, (1974) also advocated favourable, helpful and sympathetic attitude of teachers towards them. In the study of Gangrade (1974), most of the respondents were satisfied with the attitude of their teachers towards them.

Another set of studies revealed that teachers did not differ in their attitude. The teacher's attitude towards the children of each of the caste and religion group did not differ much with regard to item 'non-cooperation'. The teacher's attitude towards the children of all the social class groups did not differ very much. Rebecca (1974) also supported the findings of the earlier study and found that the average percentage of the teachers calculated for the three items of the opinionnaire, namely, intelligent, average and dull in studies, on the three scale basis of the attitude opinionnaire, do not register a wide difference in assessing the attitude of 75 per cent towards the children of each of the caste and religion group, namely, Brahmin, Sudras, Harijans and Kshatriyas excepting for a slightly lesser precentage indicated for Sudras and Harijans. The teachers expressed 45 per cent Harijan children were well behaved as compared to other caste as per the attitude of the teachers.

In the study of Felice (1977), it was found that the age old discrimination attitude of forward caste towards Harijans has not been fully eredicated. Thus caste barrier in interaction still prevails even among the modern educated youth. It is a still distant goal to integerate the scheduled caste with higher caste yeople. Many scheduled caste students complained about the adverse attitude of their higher caste classmates and one sixth of them reported about the discrimination by the society on account of their castes (Gangrade, 1974). Vagiswari (1973) also supported the findings and expressed that harejans are conscious of more discriminatory of the caste hindu. Behavioural social distance was greater in scheduled caste than attitudinal social distance. Ahmed (1980) found significant difference between the attitude of rural and urban schedaled caste and non-scehduled castes. Kamlesh also reported the significant difference in the attitude towards opposite sex among the scheduled caste and non-scheduled caste.

Some other investigations have highligted the moderate views. Singh (1982) stated that more than the half of the non-scheduled caste were willing to even mix and live together with the scheduled caste and justified the same while the scheduled castes revealed their interatednass to the Hindu community and showed ambivalent attitude towards caste hindu community. Both in urban and rural areas, they were more or less estranged from the uneducated section of their own community. Individually, they felt closer to those individuals who were of the same educational and social status irrespective of caste. The scheduled caste sample revealed a more radical attitude towards situation related to caste while caste hindu revealed a moderate position in their attitude towards the caste situation (Sen, 1982).

Education plays a vital role for changing the attitude of higher caste towards scheduled castes. Ahmed (1980) in his study reported that education exerted a favourable influence in changing the attitude of both the rural and the urban respondents of the three communities towards social institutions like family, religion, marriage caste, status of woman and family planning. It could also been seen that the traditional on look particular towards educated scheduled caste woman taking up various jobs had undergone considerable change and the attitude of the higher caste colleagues were found to be satisfactory. The education of scheduled caste woman had resulted towards marriage. The educated scheduled caste women believed in having their marriage arranged with their consents. They also revealed references of their family relationship with eminent persons and revealed their attitude towards their religion and reform (Sen, 1982). In addition to this the higher educated individual were found to in favour of widow remarriage than the less educated ones (Malik, 1979).

Self—Concept

Many studies have been conducted in this area. The results emerged from these studies are different. In the study of Rani (1981), the scheduled caste students had a low self-concept than non-scheduled caste students. Singh (1982) also found the lack of confidence among the scheduled castes. Parkash (1981) and Rangari (1981) too supported the results of the above studies and found that the upper caste children had a significantly better self-concept than the scheduled castes. In the study of Gupta, it was reported that the scheduled caste and backward classes graduate and post graduate students have significantly higher mean socres as compared to the non-scheduled castes on need affiation. The students, however, herbour in their heart, a lower level of need autonomy. Both the group have much difference on self-concept. The scheduled caste students felt themselves more inadequate and inferior in comparison to the higher castes. They also suffered more from feelings of emotional instability in comparison to non-scheduled caste students (Dogra, 1971). Sutradhar (1982) found that both the children and their fathers from advantaged group had positive self-concept, whereas in the disadvantaged group both the fathers and their children reported negative self-eoncept. The child centredness of the parents was more marked in the case of advantaged children than in the case of disadvantaed children. Naidgu (1981) conducted a study on self image of the scheduled caste youth. Three self-images of the respondents differ significantly. Incongruence had been found between the image by self image created by in-group and image created by out-group rather on the excessive side in some aspects their images is still marked by their age old social stigma.

The self-concept of both the group was studied at microlevel to the significant difference between both the group with respect to sex, place of living and other factors etc. In case of sex, Aggarwal (1982) reported that there ware statistical caste significant differences in self-concept. The girls belonging to scheduled castes had lower self-concept than Kshatriya, Brahamin and Vaish girls. The self concept of Kshatriya girls was found on the top of the hierarchy. But Rangari (1981) reported in his investigation that there was no significant differences on the self-concept between both the group.

Regarding the place of living Rangari (1981) found in his study that there was no significant difference on self-conecpt image between rural and urban areas whereas Gaur (1987) reported that non-scheduled caste boys as compared to scheduled caste and rural non-scheduled caste as compared to scheduled caste rural boys were found to be significantly higher in their overall self-concept knowledge of self variable was considered to be significant differences between rural and urban scheduled caste on economic value, social value, temperamental self-concept, social value, verbal intelligence, moral self-concept, intellectual self-concept etc. Kamalesh (1981) also supported the findings and found that non-scheduled caste students from the urban areas belonging to higher socio-econmic status had brighter self-concept than the scheduled caste students belonging to lower socio-economic status.

The economic factor also plays significant affect on the self-concept of the scheduled caste. Nagaraju (1977) conducted a study on this aspect and found that the scheduled caste come from the lowest socio-economic strata had a moderate positive self-concept. Generally they looked forward to taking up salaried jobs. Self-concept was found to be significantly related with achievement. Besides this other factors like poverty, humilating and discriminatory treatment by the teachers and classmates and a tendency to keep them under hegemony create a negative self-imang among the scheduled caste children which also hamper the progress of their education (Dogra. 1971).

Educational Aspiration

The scheduled caste aspired for educational stages in different manner. 43.25%, 23.25%, 5.75%, 2.1% and 2.5% of the students aspired to achieve bachelors, masters, law, engineering and medical degrees respectively. Another 23.25% of them wanted to have teachers training. Two third of the students hoped that they would achieve the aspired level. But SCERT (1979) reported the gap between the aspiration and actual achievement. As many as 34.4% aspired for higher education but 38.4% found higher education while the opposite held good for technical education.

Ameerjan (1984) compared scheduled caste and non-scheduled caste and found that the perception of parent's aspiration for their wards for higher education was found to be low. However, the scheduled caste students did not differ significantly from that of the other caste in their rural background and the medium of instruction. The scheduled caste by and large continue to predominate in their traditional occupation of agriculture labour. It is the urban areas that they have gained most in the salaired employment sector. The scheduled caste continue in their traditional occupation in the rural areas. Children stopped in literacy and only a small proportion of children of school gaining age attend school. Consequently they may lead to the emergence of an elite, of a small upper crust of educated and well placed individual within caste and also of chite caste among them.

In the study of Thakural (1971) it was found that the scheduled caste on the average had low level of vocational aspiration as compared to non-scheduled castes and were also low in idealistic and reatistic vocational aspiration as compared to non-scheduled castes. The same holds true in rural and urban areas (Gaur, 1987). Singh (1975) also found that these students had low level of aspiration for the technical and professional aspirations whereas chitnis (1974), Gangrade (1974) and Sachchidananda (1974) found that educational and occupational aspirations of the scheduled caste students were more or less high. They did not follow the father's education. But Nayar (1975) revealed that the occupational aspirations were related to father's education and encouragement and helf suggestion.

Malik (1979) found that large number of illiterates and less educated scheduled castes persons showed their dissatisfaction. The cause for dissatisfaction with their job may be that they were engaged in low and unclean job which did not carry any prestige in the society. The higher the level of education of the respondents, the higher were their occupational aspirations. Parents wanted to give them best education so that they can be placed in high occupation and do away with the traditional occupation. Singh (1980) emphasised that there was high correlation between educational attainments of the respondents and their current occupational status. The occupation of the father had correlation with the son's occupation.

Chand (1975) reported that the students are most influencing in choice of the subject. Most of the boys aspire for administrative, executive and similar other job. Some aspired for clerical job. The students have given the highest liking for the subjects offered by them because they believe their choice will help them in their future career. Higher achievement in examination is their best choice for their offerings. Gupta (1982) studied the vocational choices of scheduled castes and non-scheduled caste students. The scheduled caste boys indicated preferences for white collar officers vocations like (i) IAS/M.P. political top posts (ii) banking officers, Business Manager/Executive officers (iii) lawyers, advovates, journalists and editors in order of preference but the boys of non-scheduled caste have ranked the sequence of vocations from most prefence to least preferred. Joshi (1980) in his study expressed that the scheduled caste students had low aspiration and were not clear about their future but in another study it was found that the scheduled caste did not have high aspiration, did not perceive a clear aim in life and did not have a clear future career goal.

Anum Kampa (1982) compared the scheduled caste and non-scheduled caste students on vocational aspirations and found that the scheduled caste students were more interested in other vocations which their family members were not following. The aspiration of the scheduled caste students were different from the non-scheduled caste students. (ii) There was vaste difference between vocational aspiration of scheduled caste students belonging to different income level groups. Similarly difference existed in non-scheduled caste students in different socio-economic students. (iii) There was vast difference between vocational interest of scheduled caste boys and girls. (iv) There was significant difference in the degree of influence between the scheduled caste boys and girls under family factors. The girls tend to make wrong choice under the personal factors as compared to that of the boys in the scheduled caste groups as well as under the non-scheduled caste groups. (v) The scheduled caste boys tend to get more influenced by the family factors in comparison to non-scheduled caste. The scheduled caste boys get affected by social, religious, and cultural more extent than to non-scheduled caste. (vi) The scheduled caste girls tend to have greater influence of the family factor as compared to the influence on the non-scheduled caste girls. Similarly social, religious, cultural and economic factors.

Adishshia and Ramanathan (1974) found that the girls students had clean educational and professional aspirations and unlike the boys did not find teaching as difficult. Knowledge of reservation of post in government services has enhanced their occupational aspiration. Almost all students gave their first preference for the government jobs.

The above discussion related to the research reviews in the field of attitude, self-concept and aspiration level of the scheduled caste has made clear that these psychological factors play vital role in the development of child's personality and can bring fruitful results to the scheduled caste people if these are expoloited properly. With this, the increasing gaps between scheduled caste and non-scheduled caste can be decreased and the progress of scheduled caste people can also be brought equivalent to the non-scheduled caste people.

Section—B : Research Studies

This section comprised of the research studies conducted on the education for the scheduled castes. Seven research studies have been discussed and presented in this section. The studies have been conducted on intelligence, motivational aspects, vocational anxiety, teaching attitude, perception about educational chemes and their living styles. The above studies covered the sample population of scheduled caste parents, teachers and students. It helped to bring the actual state of affairs of this caste and also helped in suggesting the realistic solution for improving their status.

10

Demographic Profile of Scheduled Caste Families

Ours is a country of multillingual, multicultural, multiracial and multicastes where lot of confusions and roadblocks arise from time to time in the path of the progress of the society and the nation. Sometimes it becomes very difficult to diagnose the faults. In such a heterogeneous structure, there are some section of the society like backward classes including scheduled castes who have been suffering psychologically, socially, educationally, culturally and economically since ages. Feudilistic society never permitted them to flourish. But there are efforts by social reformers prior to independence also to ameliorate the conditions of the scheduled castes. After independence, lot of safeguards and benefits were provided in the Constitution of the country. Many commissions and committees set up by Govt. of India and focussed the attention towards the improvement of the conditions of the scheduied caste. In new education policy also there is lot of emphasis on the education of the scheduled castes. It refers that.

The central focus in the scheduled caste's educational development is their equalisation with the non-scheduled caste population at all statesand levels of education, in all areas and in all the four dimensions—rural male, rural female, urban male and urban female.

(i) Incentives to indigent families to send their children to school regularly till they reach the age of 14.

(ii) Pre-matric scholarship scheme for children of families engaged in occupations such as scavenging, flaying and tanning to be made applicable from Class I onwards. All children of such families, regardless of their incomes, will be covered by this scheme and time—bound programmes targetted on them will be undertaken.

(iii) Constant micro—planning and verification to ensure that the enrolement, retention and successful completion of courses by SC students do not fall at any stage, and provision of remedial courses to improve their prospects for further education and employment.

(iv) Recruitment of teachers from Scheduled Castes.

(v) Provision of facilities for scheduled castes students in students hostels at district headquarters, according to phased programme.

(vi) Location of school buildings, Balwadis and Adult Education Centres in such a way as to facilitate full participation of the Scheduled Castes.

(vii) The utilisation of NREP and R.L.E.G.P. resources so as to make substantial educational facilities available to the scheduled castes and

(viii) Constant innovation in finding new methods to increase the participants of the Scheduled Castes in the educational process (NPE, 1986). Besides this, several other schemes have been introduced for the improvement of social, economic and educational status of these people. Progress has also been noticed due to these efforts in different sectors. The literacy rates of the Scheduled Castes were 10.77%,

14.67% and 21.38% respectively in 1961, 1971 and 1981, thus gaining an increase of 4.4 per cent in 1971 over 1961 and 6.71% increase in 1981 over 1971. Similar efforts have been made in economic sectors and allocations have been increased in every plan and various developmental programmes have been framed for these people. About 11.20 lakh families crossed the poverty line under the project Integerated Rural Development Project. The social status have also increased. The untouchability has also decreased to the minimum in most part of the country. The employment among these people have also increased due to these various efforts made by the Government. The amelioration of the socio-economic conditions of the Scheduled Castes depends on the actual utilisation of the schemes, programmes and services planned for them. What is the extent of coverage ? Who are the effective beneficiaries? In other words how well are the schemes distributed in the scheduled caste population? How for have they been benefitted? What are the changes effected in their lifestyle? Are we satisfied with quantum of change and the pace at which it has taken place? If not, what are the gaps? Where have we failed ? What are the achievements? In what respect have we succeeded? What can be done to streamline the plans and programmes for them so that the gains from each of the schemes converge on the quality of life at par with what is envisaged for any Indian citizen? These are some of the questions which need a microprobe. Answer to these questions will provide insight into the problems of this set of our population and the ways of tackling the same. The present study is an attempt in this direction.

Objectives

To study the perceptions of the scheduled caste children

as well as their parents towards the educational, occupational, social and economic status in the society.

Methodology and Procedure

The study followed survey technology and ethnographic excursion was preferred to cross sectional survey for the microscopic view of the problem. It is basically a survey of the perception and opinion of the heads of the family and their children with respect to the respectability in the society in form of social, economic, educational and occupational status. The problems and issues related to the above areas have been covered in this study. This section is devoted to the sampling procedure, tool used, data collection and analysis carried out.

Sample

Multistage sampling was used. At first the localities where scheduled caste families were living with thick population both in rural and urban areas were identified with the help of Census, 1981. Then the local community leaders were identified and were contracted so that study can be conducted in a free and congenial atmosphere. They provided us the list of the families and their heads. Out of the list of 500 families, 25 were picked up by draw of lots We also used the good offices of the community leaders for establishing report with these families.

Tool Used

The draft tool on Family Information Schedule (FIS) was prepared. This tool was sent to ten experts working in the area alongwith list of objectives of the study to give their opinion about the adequacy and appropriatness of questions. They were also requested to suggest modifications, additions or deletion of the questions. On the basis of their judgement the questionnaire was tried out and refined. The questionnarire was semi-structured for collecting information on different aspects of family life. The demographic information was totally structured. FIS was like Census performa covering all living members of the family right from birth. The age of the members of the family, sex, relation with heads of family, and marital status of the family members constituted first section. The structured part also included information about the educational, occupational and social status of every members of the family. The questions regarding the explainatory information about different parameters envisaged in the study constituted the unstructured segment of the schedule. The parametres included their views about the size of the family, their opinion about the education, and the means of livelihood they adopted.

Data Collection

Case studies of twenty five families were conducted. The scheduled caste localities in Delhi both from rural and urban areas were identified with the help of last Census report. The report with the local community leaders were established, for establishing link with these families. Before embarking on venture, we strengthened our social bonds through frequent visits, sharing of cups of tea and glasses of water which proved miraculus in breaking the barrier to communication by reducing social distance. FIS was administered to these families. Face to face interaction with the heads of family was the major source of information. We also interact with the family members whenever possible.

Analysis and Interpretation

The present study followed survey technology and is discriptive in nature. Percentage analysis was carried out in this study.

Findings

The significant findings emerging from the study are given below:

The Parents

Out of twenty five families, twenty three males as the heads of the family, while in the remaining two, the fathers had expired and mothers acted as the heads of the family. The age of the fathers ranged from 42 years to 67 years with an average of 49.6 years, while the age of the mothers range from 38 years. Obviously, the mothers are younger in age than the fathers. The difference are quite significant. This is the result of the social convention arising out of the belief that the bridegroom is to be senior in age to the brids. It is also based on the cultural generalisation arising from the differentiated maturation rates of the males and females, particularly in early years. The early marriages prevalent in our society takes it into account for marriage purposes. Another reason for this discripancy is economic. The male spouse being the bread earner with a protective fold around the female spouse, the seniority in age is also kept up.

The Children

The population of the children was 194 consisting of 108 boys and 86 girls. The age range varies from one and half year to 35 years with an average of 14 years.

Table 10.1

Age of the Children

(*N*=194)

Age Range	*Total No. of the Children*	*Percentage*
0–6	18	9.2%
6—11	34	17.5%
11—14	29	14.9%
14—18 & above	113	58.2%

Differentially 18 (9.2%) Children fall in the 0—6 age group, 34 (17.5%) Children in 6—11 years, 29 (14.9%)

Children in 11—14 years and 113 (58.2%) Children in 14.18 years.

Family Size

The total member of the children in the families covered comes to 194 (108 boys and 86 girls). The average family size in the set covered in the study comes to 9.8 which is almost one and a half times more than the national average family size of 6.2 Differentiated on the basis of the location of the family, it is a little higher in the case of rural based families having an average of 10.2 than the urban based families having an average of 9.4. It implies that some families do have the size larger than the average. The families covered in the investigation have more boys than girls, predictably, due to the higher survival rate among male children against the survival among the female children.

Occupation

Most the parents and their children were working as Safai Karamchari, maid servants, peons, feeding the cattle, repairs the shoes, cycle, turner, salesman, chokidar, and unskilled labours etc. Very few persons were working as clerks, U D.C. or Assistant and teachers etc. in government departments. The occupations were catergorised in four broad categories, namely, services comprising Class IV, Class III, Class II and Class I, agriculture comrising landless agricultural labour, share cropping, own land small farming, own land large farming; industry comprising unskilled labour through skilled labour, supervisory and manegerial to executive position; trade comprising vending through relating and wholesaling to enterpreneuring.

From the above table, it is clear that out of the 242 individuals comprising the twenty five families, 62 (25.5%) members are working and other are not engaged in any occupations either they are studing or unemployed. A few of them are below teenages. Differentially, out of the sixty two, one (0.01%) is engaged in Class I services, three (0.04%) in

Table 10.2

Occupational Pattern of the Family

(N = 242)

Category	*No. of the Persons*	*Percentage*
Services		
Class I	1	0.01%
Class II	3	0.04%
Class III	7	0.11%
Class IV	16	0.25%
Industry		
Skilled Labour	2	0.03%
Unskilled Labour	26	0.41%
Business		
Ratail Shopping	3	0.04%
Vendors	4	0.06%
Total	62	0.25%

Class II services, seven (0.11%) in Class III services and 16 (0.25%) in Class IV services. Two (0.03%) and twenty six (0.41%) are involved in skilled and unskilled labour in industtial establishment. Three (0.04%) of them are involved in retail shopping while four (0.06%) of them are vendor. Obviously, in services, majority of them are in the lowest rung. In industries, the largest number is engaged in unskilled labour. None of them has reached supervisory level in industries and no one has been able to travel beyond retail shopping in business. Surprising enough, one figured in agriculture despite the fact that some rural locations were covered. It is mainly due to the fact that these family members even from rural areas, manage to find employment in government semi-government establishments and industrial concerns where they feel more comfortable and more service socially. Once in these organisations, the social prejudice starts declining.

Economic Profile

The Table 10.3 provides information about the average monthly income, per capita income, yearly per capita income and national per capita income.

Table 10.3

Economic Profile of the Family

(*N* = 25)

Category	*Income*	*National Per Capita Income*
Average monthly Income	878.20	1749.50
Per Capita Income	92.00	
Yearly per Capita Income	964.00	

The families included in this investigation have been able to generate an average monthly income of Rs. 873.20 per month which sounds quite optimistic when compared to other such families in other part of the country. But the optimism pales into insignificance when it is considered in terms of per capita income which comes to Rs. 92.00 per month. Yearly per capita income comes out to be Rs. 964.00 which is much below the average national per capita income of Rs. 1794.50. The income of this group of families and individuals continues to be much below the national average. The gap between the two appears to have become perennial showing signs of stagnation. On the face of it the situation appears to have been impreving but in reality, it is either stagnant or deteriorating. One of the main reasons is the larger number of mouths created for feeding. But for this reason, the situation might have been much optimistic.

Educational Scenario

The income generating capabilities depend on education and training of the work force. It is, therefore, essentially necessary to study the educational set up of these families.

Table 10.4

Education of the Parents

N = 23 (Father)
N = 25 (Mother)

S N.	*Category*	*Percents*	*Percentage*
1.	*Father*		
	Graduate	1	4.3%
	Matriculate	5	21.7%
	Middle	1	4.3%
	Primary	2	8.6%
	Literate	2	8.6%
	Illiterate	12	52.1%
2.	*Mother*		
	Primary	1	4.0%
	Illiterate	24	96%

Out of the twenty three male heads of the family (Fathers) only one (4.3%) is gradutate, five (21.7%) matriculates, one (4.3%) Middle pass, two (8.5%) primary pass, the other two (8.6%) can read and write, and twelve (52.1%) are illiterate. Out of the twenty five mothers twenty four (96%) are illiterate and only one (4%) is primary pass. Obviously, the educational level of the parents in these families is very low. This is mainly because of the reason that they belong to a generation which had been very litited educational opportunity, and whatever facilities were available, they could not utilise due to sociopsychological barriers to the extent that the educational reach had been quite difficult. We are constrained to point out the failure of our adult education programme.

The Children

The table shows the educational scene of the children of these twenty five families.

Table 10.5

Education Profile of the Children

(N = 194)

Category	*No. of the Children*	*Percentage*
Attending	66	34.02%
Non-Attending	76	39.1%
Drop-out	36	18.5%
Not-eligible	16	8.2%
Total	194	100%

Out of the 194 children habitating the families in question, 16 (8.2%) children are not eligible as they have yet to reach the age of six years. Only 66 children (34.02%) are in the educational pipeline, while 76 (39.1%) are non attending which implies that they have never been to the school and 36 (18.5%) children have been dropped out.

Drop-out

Drop-out means children who withdraw themselves prematuraly from any stages. Thirty six children dropped out from the educational system at different stages.

Out of the thirty six dropouts, 14 (38.8%) dropped out from the primary stages comprising I to V, 17 (47.2%) from the middle school comprising VI to VII and 5 (13.8%)

Table 10.6

Percentage of Drop-out in Different Stages

(N = 36)

S.N.	*Stage*	*No. of the Children*	*Percentage*
1.	Primary	14	38.8%
2.	Middle	17	47.2%
0.	Secondary	5	13.8%
	Total	36	1C0.00%

dropped out at the secondary stage comprising classes IX to XII. The lower dropout rate at primary stage is due to the fact that large number of the children did not attend the school at all. Most of these children continue their studies upto primary level, but the dropout increases sharply at the middle stage mostly as a result of frustration arising out of stagnation and active involvement in income generating activities. Very limited dropout at secondary stage is due to the low survival rate upto middle stage. Those who servive continue to the secondary stage.

It is evident from the excursion that educational status of the families is extremaly low with few exceptions. The low enrolment and heavy dropout rate are indicators of this disturbing trend. What is more disturbing is that none of the child has been touched by the programme of non-formal education otherwise, is reported have made signification progress during the last decades.

Attending Children

The Table—provides the information about the attending children.

Table 10.7

Education Scene of the Attending Children

(N = 66)
Male = 42
Female = 24

S.N.	*Category*	*No. of the Children*	*Percentage*
1.	*Male*		
	Literate (can read & write)	2	4.7 %
	Primary	19	45.2 %
	Middle	13	30.9 %
	Secondary & Beyonded	8	19.09%
2.	*Female*		
	Literate	1	4.1 %
	Primary	17	62.5 %
	Middle	4	16.6 %
	Secondary & Above	2	8.3 %

The above Table provided the clear picture of the attending male and female children. In both the categories, the maximum children are at primary stages. After the primary stage, the male children generally engage in supplementing the income of the family and the female children either looks after the younger children at home or helps her mother. Social evils are also the cause for not sending the female children after this stage.

Family Welfare Profile

Most of the parents and their children are not knowing the welfare programme for their upliftment regarding social, economic, occupational and educational status provided by the government. It is due to the faulty procedure of the publicity. The people from urban areas are utilising more welfare benefits than the rural areas. It is also for the easy availability of the publicity media than the rural areas.

The examination of the above twenty five families shows that most of the parents as well as children are illiterate and confined by so many social evils but in some educated families the picture is totally different. These families have improved their social, economic, occupational and their living standards. They have also become confident and self reliant socially, psychologically, economically and culturally.

11

Cognitive and Motivational Level of Scheduled Caste and Non-Scheduled Caste Students

The scheduled castes, the large size of the population, have been suffering since ages. Though various efforts were made to improve their lot specially after independence but even then these is wide gap between scheduled castes and higher castes. It means the present efforts and the constitutional safeguards are not enough. In order to show better results it would be necessary to investigate the causes of their backwardness and then eliminate these causes to remove their backwardness with the help of research studies. The present study is an attempt in this direction. It seeks to investigate two important factors of learning, viz. motivational tendencies and intelligence level in the scheduled caste in comparison to non-scheduled caste population.

Very few studies have been conducted to investigate the motivational tendencies and intellectual capacity of socially backward classes. The studies of Bradburn, (1963); Cameron, (1965); Poussaint Alvin, (1868); Hines (1973); Minigion, (1965) and Mossback, (1969) proved that the coloured population is inferior in Achievement Motivation. But the studies of Burial, (1966); Hall, (1975); Prayag Mehta, (1967); Minigione,

(1963); Julka, (1963) and Amita, Choksi (1975) found no such discriminations.

Objective

The present study was taken with the following aims:

1. To compare the intelligence level of the scheduled caste and non-scheduled caste students.
2. To compare the motivational tendencies of the students belonging to these two categories.

Design of the Study

(i) *Statement of the Problem*

A Comparative Study of the Intelligence level and the Motivational Tendeneies of the Scheduled Caste and Non-Scheduled Caste Students.

(ii) *Hypotheses*

1. The scheduled caste and non-scheduled caste students do not differ significantly in any of the sentiment measured by Motivational Analysis Test, Viz., Career sentiment, home-parental sentiment, fear (escape) erg, Narcissm comfort erg, super ego sentiment, self-concept sentiment, mating erg, pugnacity sadism erg, assertiveness of erg, and sweet heart spouse sentiment.
2. There is no significant difference in the intelligence level of the scheduled caste and non-scheduled caste students.

(iii) *Sample*

The population in the case of the present study has been defined as the scheduled caste and non-scheduled caste students in the district of Ajmer. The sample of 50 students from each group was drawn for the purposes of the study. Out of 79 schools in this district two urban schools were randomly selected for the study. As the students of IX and X were easily available, the study was confined to the students of class IX and X. Thus the sample of the study consisted of 100 students, details of which are given below :

Sr. No.	*School*	*Number of students of scheduled caste*	*Number of non-scheduled caste students*
1.	Mahatma Gandhi Higher Secondary School, Ajmer	34	15
2.	Husband Memorial Higher Secondary School, Ajmer	16	35
	Total	50	50

(iv) *Tools used*

To collect data the following tools were used :

1. Raven's Standard Progressive Matrices test for measuring intelligence factor.
2. Motivational Analysis test by Dr. Kpoor and Dr. Singh for the purpose of assissing motivational factors.

The selection of Raven's Standard Progressive Matrices was due to the following considerations.

Standard Progressive Matrics has been widely used in this country and enjoys a good degree of reputation. Test-retest reliability of the test as worked out by Raven varies from persons in different age ranges but never goes down below 83. Raven also provides satisfactory relationship of this test with Mill Hill vocabulary scales and Term an Merril Intelligence Quotient. Mason worked out .90 as the reliability co-efficient. Desai sound its split-half reliability to be .89.

Motivational Analysis Test

There are a number of tests measuring various aspects of motivation separately. If the investigator has used these tests to measure various aspects of motivation in scheduled caste and non-scheduled caste students, it would have become too much time consuming. Motivational Analysis Test of Kapoor and Ram Nayan Singh is an adaptation of a test developed by the Institute for Personality and Ability testing, U.S.A. It measures ten aspects of motivation and is quite comprehensive on coverage. The investigator administered the Motivational Analysis test by Dr. Shayamji Dass Kapoor and Dr. Ram Nayan Singh, 1973 (Hindi Edition) for getting scores on verious dimensions of motivation. It offers special advantages in regard to comparative and development research. The school motivational analysis test is meant for the age range from eleven to seventeen years. The test has been found to have quite adequate reliability and validity for each ten M.A.T. Scales. These aspects and their operational definitions as given in the manual are geven below.

Sr. No.	*Title*	*Brief description*
1.	Career Sentiment	Amount of development of interest in a carrer.
2.	Assertiveness erg	Strength of the drive to self-assertion mastery and achievement.
3.	Fear (Escape) erg	Level of alertness to external dangers (This is not anxiety).
4.	Narcism comfort erg	Level to drive to sensuous, self-indulgent satisfactions.
5.	Superego sentiment	Strength of development of conscience.
6.	Self-concept sentiment	Level of concern about the self-concept social repute and more remote rewards.

Sr. No.	*Title*	*Brief description*
7.	Mating erg	Strength of the normal, hetro-sexual or mating drive.
8.	Punguncity-sadisim erg	Strength of destructive hostee impulses.
9.	Home parental sentiment	Strength of attitudes attaching to the parental home.
10.	Sweet heart—spouse sentiment	Strength of attachment to wife (husband) or sweet-heart.

(v) *Analysis of Data and Results*

The method used after collecting raw scores was to convert them into stanine score and then Mann-Whitney U-Test was used to find differences in the frequency distributions of stanine scores in various aspects of motivation among scheduled caste and non-scheduled caste students. Similarly C.R. Test was used to test the significance of the difference in the intelligence level of these two groups. Results of the Mann-Whitney U-Test (Seigal Sidney 1956) are given in the Table 11.1.

Result of the C.R. Test to the hypothesis No. 2 are given in Table. 11.2.

C.R. Test value, being not singnificant, the hypothesis could not be rejected.

Discussion of the Results

The findings of the study, have revealed that there is no significant difference between scheduled caste and non-scheduled caste students on intelligence level and motivational tendencies. So far as distribution of intelligence is concerned,

Table 11.1

Results of Mann-Whitney U-Test

No.	Demension	Total Rank Scheduled Caste R_1	Total Rank Non-Schedled Caste R_2	U	Z	Significance
1.	Career Sentiment	2672.0	2378.0	1103.0	—1.0267	N.S.
2.	Home partental sentiment	2720.0	2340.0	1055.0	—1.362	N.S.
3.	Fear (Escape) erg	2410 5	2639.5	1364.5	.789	N.S.
4.	Naricism-comfort erg	2643.5	2448.5	1131.5	.817	N S.
5.	Super ego sentiment	2610 5	2439.5	1164.5	.589	N.S.
6.	Self concept sentiment	2631.0	2420.5	1144.0	.7303	N.S.
7.	Mating erg	2339.5	2710.5	1445.5	1.298	N.S.
8.	Pugnacity-sadism erg	2464.5	2579 0	1310 5	.417	N.S.
9.	Assertiveness	2432.6	2856.0	1342 5	.637	N.S.
10.	Sweet heart spouse Sentiment	2412.5	2193 50	1362.5	.775	N.S.

Table 11.2

Resuslt of C.R. Test

Scheduled Caste M_1	*Non-Scheduled Caste M_2*	*Difference*	*Standard error of the mean*	*C.R.*	*Level of significance*
33.7	32.85	0.85	1.09	77.	N.S.

nature has not been unduly fair or unfair to any category of people. Moreover, the scheduled caste students have the same motivations as the non-scheduled caste students have. Thus it is evident that scheduled caste students are not inferior to non-scheduled caste students in any respect. For their low achievement and performance, there may be other reasons. So no student should ever be rejected for any job, simply on the basis of his brith in a scheduled caste family.

12

Vocational Anxiety Among Scheduled Caste Pupil Tegchers

The 20th century has rightly been described as the age of anxiety. There is no denying the fact that numerous problems of mankind have been solved by tremendous scientific progress and technological advancement. But it is also true that technology is getting priority over humanity in the modern world. Instead of improving the quality of life, it has increased considerably the tensions and conflicts which certainly make full functioning of an individual's personality difficult.

Pleasures and pains of life actually depend upon the inner state of the organism. Every aspect of our environment appears enjoyable to us if we are happy at heart, whearas we are in a mood to despise all the things if we are unhappy at heart. Unhappiness, sadness, irritation and a number of other unpleasant states of life are most evident outcomes of anxiety.

Anxiety producing factors are either present in the personality of an individual or these may be present in the situation in which he is placed at a particular time. A person will be said to have general anxiety if anxiety producing states are a part and parcel of his total personality. In otherwords, it can be said that he will have anxious disposition or anxiety proness, that is, he will be temperamentally anxious person. On the other hand, if an individual experiences anxiety for not having been able to meet the demands of a situation adequately, then he is said to have experienced situational anxiety.

It is a matter of common knowledge that teacher trainees have to face a number of such problems as are peculiar to teacher training institutions along. Some of them really intend to become teachers in their later lives but there are many other who simply wish to remain busy for one more year and thus plan to get time to find some more suitable job. On being admitted to a teacher training college, they find themselves in a 'New Land' with which they were not familiar in their previous institutions. They are required to study for longer hours and are subjected to strict and rigid discipline of secondary schools. They are called upon to study altogether new subjects and participate in the programme of student teaching and discussion lessons. Besides, fear of future unemployment and resultant low status in family and society, keeps haunting their minds. These are some of the factors which make the student teachers anxious in the situation in which they have placed themselves willingly or unwillingly, happily or unhappily. The specific or situational anxiety experienced by teacher-trainees has been labelled as Vocational Anxiety. It implies the anxiety experienced by teacher trainees with reference to their present educational status and future professional or employment status.

Lal, (1974) studied vocational anxiety in relation to general anxiety and teaching success and found that vocational anxiety has a separate entity and these two types of anxiety are not reducible to one. The same study revealed that vocational anxiety is negatively related to teaching success. Arora, (1976) studied the relationship between vocational anxiety and creative thinking ability and discovered that the two are curvilinearly related to each other. This implies that high as well as low anxiety go with low creativity, whereas middle level anxiety provides scope for optimum functioning of creative potential. Kumari, (1978) found that vocational anxiety is negatively related to both academic achievement and teaching aptitude. Thus, it implies that vocational anxiety is linked with low teaching competence as well as low academic achievement. Therefcre it becomes necessary to study to Phenomenon of vocational anxiety in order to ascertain which segments of the teacher trainees are more vulnerable to vocational anxiety and which are less vulnerable. This is rightly the genesis of the present study. The significance of the study lies in the fact that its findings will certainly go a long way in providing guidance services to the trainees experiencing vocational anxiety.

Objectives

It is matter of common observation that all the teacher trainees do not form a homogeneous group. They differ from each other with regard to sex, place of living socio-economic background, educational background etc. etc. As stated above, the main aim of the present investigation is to ascertain which groups of teacher trainees experience more vocational anxiety than the others. More specifically, the objectives of the study can be listed as under :

(i) To as certain whether men and women teacher trainees differ from each other significantly in mean performance on the test of vocational anxiety.

(ii) To determine whether parental occupation has some sort of linkage with vocational anxiety.

(iii) To ascertain whether trainees with science subjects differ significantly from other trainees with regard to vocational anxiety.

(iv) To ascertain whether trainees coming from rural areas differ significantly in vocational anxiety from the trainees belonging to urban areas.

(v) To determine whether previous teacher training is linked with vocational anxiety.

(vi) To determine the relationship between vocational anxiety and age of the trainees.

(vii) To determine the relationship between vocational anxiety and performance of the trainees in the qualifying examination.

Sample

The sample of the study comprised 159 scheduled caste teacher trainees drawn from the colleges of Education in Haryana.

Collection of Data

Dr. Arora's vocational anxiety scale (1976) was selected to measure vocational anxiety in the sample population. The scale comprises 44 items in which admit three alternative responses. A score of two is assigned to a response indicating presence of vocational anxiety, whereas a response indicating its absence is assigned a score of zero. A non-commital response is assigned the score of one. The scale has proved to be reliable and valid tool for the measurement of vocational anxiety. The scale was administered to teacher trainees in colleges in sizeable groups. Proper conditions for the administration of psychological tests were fully taken care of.

Statistical Analysis

In the first instance, it was decided to explore the possibility of differences in mean performance on the test of vocational anxiety in respect of different categories of teacher trainees. The 't' test was employed to sest the significance of differences between means. Pearson product moment coefficient of correlation was computed in order to ascertain the relationship of vocational anxiety with previous academic achievement and age of the trainees. Table 12.1 depicts comparative position of different categories of teacher trainees in mean performance on vocational anxiety scale. Product moment coefficients of correlation between vocational anxiety scores, age and academic achievement scores are given in Table 12.1.

Table 12.1
Significance of Difference in Mean Vocational Anxiety Scores

Categories	*N*	*Mean*	*N*	*Mean*	*D Mean*	*Sed*	*E*
A. *Mother's Occupation*	6	28.16	153	33.94	5.78	1.368	4 2**
(i) Service (ii) Housewife							
B. *Father's Occupation*							
(i) Service (ii) Agriculture	69	31.75	39	35.5	3.75	.66	5.6**
(i) Service (ii) Business	69	31.75	51	34.85	3 10	.59	5.2**
(i) Business (ii) Agriculture	51	34.85	39	35.5	.65	.70	.92
C. *Subjects*							
(i) Arts (ii) Science	137	35.35	22	31.90	3.45	.47	4.6**
D. *Place of Livings*							
(i) Rural (ii) Urban	63	32.5	96	31.90	.60	.46	1.3*
E. *Sex*							
(i) Male (ii) Female	41	36.60	118	32.35	4.25	.578	7.3
F. *Previous Training*							
(i) Fresh (ii) Trained	146	33.80	13	30.15	3.65	.952	3.8

* Significance at .05 Level
** Significance at .01 Level

Table 12.2

Significance of Product Moment Coefficients of Correlation

	Variables	*r*	*df*	*p*
1.	Vocational Anxiety and Age of the Trainees	.09	157	n.s.
2.	Vocational Anxiety and Academic Achievement	.22	157	.01

Results and Discussion

1. Teacher trainees whose mothers are working ladies experience less vocational anxiety than the trainees whose mothers are only housewives. This finding is obviously along with expected lines. The children of working mothers perhaps know the hazards of such jobs from the beginning of their life. They perhaps get hardened due to lack of over protection by parents. However, this finding needs further support from more research studies as the number of working mothers included in the sample of the present study is very small.
2. Table 12.1 reveals that the teacher trainees whose fathers are in service, are less prone to vacational anxiety than the trainees whose fathers are in business or agriculture. This finding is again alongwith expected lines. The children whose fathers are in service generally reconcile to the fact that they have no other alternative but to go in for service. The children whose fathers are in business or agriculture, have informal training in these occupations. Moreover, these occupations are a part of their home environment. They opt for a service career either because of alteraction for white collared jobs or disliking for businsss or agriculture. Lack of initial training and the conflicts concerning choice of careers, make them more prone to vocational anxiety. As occupations business and agriculture have a number of common

points, that is why, trainees whose fathers are in business do not differ significantly in vocational anxiety from the trainees whose fathers are in agriculture.

3. Table 12.1 reveals that trainees with science subjects differ significantly in vocational anxiety from the trainees with other subjects. They experience less anxiety because they know that they will some how get jobs after completing the training. Moreover, they were used to working for longer hours in their previous institutions also.
4. The study has revealed that vocational anxiety has got no linkage with place of living. This implies that the trainees belonging to rural areas do not experience more or less vocational anxiety than the urbanites. Both the groups may have their peculiar problems but the same donot appear to be related to vocotional anxiety.
5. A large number of studies have confirmed that women experience more enxiety than men. But in the case of vacational anxiety, the present study has revealed that it is the male trainees who experience more vocational anxiety. This can be attributed to the fact that male trainees are more serious about getting a job after the training. Their status in the family and society will depend on their being employed adequately. They are always aware that their future employment status will largely depend on the outcome of their success in the various programmes of the teacher training college. On the other hand, most of the female trainees join the training class simply to acquire some sort of professional qualification.
6. It is clear from Table 12.1 that the trainees with previous teacher training experience less vocational anxiety than the fresh graduates. This implies that previous teaching experience and teacher training make them favourably towards teaching profession. They acquire the skills required for taking up a teaching job. However, this finding needs to be further verified because of small number of such teachers in the sample of the present study.

7. Table 12.2 reveals that the product moment coefficient of correlation (r) between vocational anxiety and age of the trainees is .09, which is not statistically significant. Thus it has become clear that no linkage exists between these two variables, that is, age of the trainees has nothing to do with vocational anxiety.
8. It is clear from Table 12.2 that the product moment coefficient of correlation (r) between vocational anxiety and previous academic achievement is —.22, which is significant at .01 level of significance. The negative relationship confirms that high academic achievement is a function of high level of intelligence, whereas low achievement is not due to low intelligence alone. Adequate level of intelligence and high academic achievement equip a person with confidence which is essential for facing a new situation.

Educational Implications

The study has some important implications for the selection of teacher trainees belonging to scheduled caste for admission to B.Ed class and also for the need of providing guidance services for such students in the teacher training institutions. Level of achievement at the qualifying examination and previous teacher training teaching experience should be given due weightage in the criterion for admission to B.Ed. class. Guidance services must be provided to the trainees who are found to be experiencing highlevel of vocational anxiety. In the absence of adequate guidance services, their maladjustment may get worsened, which may affect their academic achievement and teaching competence adversely.

13

Teacher's Perception on Educational Schemes

The Context

Education occupies a place of significance in the U.N. Charter of Human Rights. The author of the Indian Constitution justifiably recognised the need for universal elementary education in the age group 6—14 in a bid to develop an egalitarian society. The post independence period, therefore, has witnessed unprecedented expansion of elementary education with consequent expansion at subsequent stages. (MEC 1983). The benefits of this expansion, however, have been differentially distributed in different sections of the society. The weaker sections, particularly the Scheduled Castes who started with the socio-economic lag of centuries, has difficult task ahead in the process of educating themselves.

The educational planners were alive to the need to provide catelyst to accelarate the pace of educational development amongst Scheduled Castes by way of different incentives constituting the educational schemes. These schemes were directed towards enrolment and retention of Scheduled Castes children in the system. Despite these schemes, the situation is far from satisfactory. The enrolment ratio in the case of scheduled castes children are still much lower than that in the general population. The dropout and stagnation is also quite high in these children (Yadav, 1983). It raises several questions. Are the educational schemes adquate ? Is their implementation faulty ? If so, what are the shortcomings and in what ways can they be overcome ? Some studies have been conducted to seek answers to the questions posed above. Sachchidananda, (1974) suggested that welfare schemes for the Harijans should be periodically evaluated. Lal, (1974) suggested to study the condition of the Harijans groups which are not able to use facilities provided by the Government. The difficulties in availing of the scheme were to be identified. Naik, (1971); Gangrade, (1974); Parvathama. (1974) and Pimply, (1974); also conducted empirical studies of various aspects of educational schemes for Harijans. Yadav, (1983) studied the awareness of parents of the Scheduled Caste children about the schemes and their perception of problems in availing these schemes. The study also covered students' awareness. It was considered desirable to study the teachers perception of the educational schemes. their utilisation, short-coming and suggestions for improving the same to increase their effectiveness. Most of these studies have focused on parents and students perceptions of the scheme. Teachers perceptions have been ignored hitherto. The present study was designed to fill this long felt gap in investigations relating to this area.

Objectives

The specific objectives of the study can be stated as under :

1. To identify the educational schemes aiming at facilitating education of the children belonging to scheduled castes.
2. To study the perception of the teachers regarding the educational schemes directed at facilitating education of the children belonging to Scheduled Castes.

3. To study the teacher's perception of the problems which they face in utilising the educational schemes for facilitating the education of their children.
4. To study the directions for procedural modifications with a view to facilitating utilisation of the educational schemes by the scheduled caste with particular perference to the conditions of eligibility, value of scholarships, selection of condidates, duration and renewal of awards, mode of payment, mode of publicity and submitting application.
5. To study the problems of these students belonging to scheduled castes who do not avail the educational benefits/facilities despite being eligible for them.
6. To study the causes of the drop-out of students belonging to scheduled castes and remedial steps to arrest the same.
7. To study the teacher's perception of the academic achievement of the scheduled castes.

Methodology and Procedure

The study followed survey methodology. It is basically a survey of the perception ond opinion of the teachers with respect to the educational schemes of the scheduled castes and their management at different levels. The problems and issues involved have also been covered. This section is devoted to the sampling procedure, toolused, data collected and analysis carried out.

Sample

Multistage sampling was followed for the study. At the first stage schools constituted the population. Fifty primary schools and twenty secondary schools were selected using the table of random number from the list of primary school procured from the department of education, Municipal Corporation and lists of secondary schools supplied by Delhi Administration, Delhi. At the second stage four teachers from each of the fifty primary schools and five from each of the secondary schools were slected randomly.

Tools Used

The draft tool was prepared by the investigator and sent to ten experts working in the areas along with a list of the objectives of the study to give their opinion about the adequacy and appropriateness of questions. They were also requested to suggest modifications additions or deletions of the questions. On the basis of their judgement the questionnaire was refined. The questionnaire was tried out with twenty teachers in twenty schools. The questionnaire was further refined for final administration. The final questionnaire contains 21 items and is divided into five broad sections. The first section includes demographic data, educational qualifications and their experience of teaching; the second section covers teachers knowledge of the schemes, perception sufficiency and utility of schemes related to their study and problems in getting loans and aids to meet the cost of education. This section also covers the problems faced by the scheduled castes in utilisation of the schemes and suggested solutions for removing difficulties in the utilisation of the schemes/facilities. The problems and suggestions cover the conditions of eligibility, mode of publicity, mode of payment, renewal of scholarships, precedure for submitting applications, award of facilities and adequacy of scholarships and other facilities/schemes under educational schemes, administration and implementation of the schemes. The third section covers teacher's opinion about such students who are eligible for the various educational facilities but not availing these facilities deliberately. The fourth section includes teacher's views about the drop-out scheduled caste students and steps to reduce it. The last section covers the academic performance of scheduled caste students in comparison to other students, for their failure or low academic performance, reasons for their lack of interest in their studies and possible solutions.

Data Collection

With permission from the Heads of institution the teachers were approached for filling up the questionnaires. The investigator explained the purpose of the study and the utilisation of its findings. The questionnaire were collected after a week from the teachers.

Analysis and Interpretation

The present study follows survey technology and is descriptive in nature. Percentage analysis of teachers perception was carried out.

Findings

The significant findings emerging from the study are given below :

1. Most of the class teachers reported that the students from their classes were availing of the educational schemes, while a few teachers reported that none of the students was availing of any of the educational schemes for their education.
2. The highest percentage of the teachers seems to be aware of the ancilliary services particularly free supply of books and uniforms. It is followed by the scholarship at pre-matric stage, post-matric scholarship and reimbursement of examination fees each. There seems to be level of awareness in schemes in which the teachers are not directly involved.
3. Sixty two per cent teachers reported that scheduled castes students can continue their education without these educational facilities and schemes while 38% teachers expressed that scheduled caste students cannot continue their studies without these schemes.
4. As many as 55.33% teachers opined that the scheduled castes students could continue their study with some difficulty if these educational schemes

are not available while about one third of teachers felt that they could continue their studies with ease without the educational schemes. Only fourteen per cent of the teachers felt that they could continue their studies with great difficulty without these educational schemes and benefits.

5. The respondents expressed different reasons for inability to continue with studies. An overwelming majority of the teachers reported that the scheduled castes children generally work in factories, tea shops and are engaged in small occuptions to help in supplementary the family income and also to cover the expenses of their studies which create hindrances in the study while sixty seven per cent teachers considered poverty and economic reasons for not continuing their studies. Corelessness of parents, inferiority complex in children, parents illiterarcy, biased behaviour of teachers, parental occupational a social habits of parents, uncongenial environment of home, belief in superstition, bad company of the children, and malnutrition, were the other reasons expressed by the respondents for not continuing their studies.

6. Forty per cent respondents expressed that the facilities and incentives available at present are quite inadequate while one their of the teachers expressed that scholarships and stipends meet the cost of study partly. One fourth of the teachers were of opinion that this cover the full cost of their education.

7. Part-time work has emerged as the chief mode of meeting the additional cost of education. It is followed by private loan on heavy interest. Some of them manage funds from charitable source for this purpose.

8. The respondents expressed that the scheduled castes are engaged in part-time work like tuition work,

milk selling, paper bags making working at tea stalls hotels, distribution of newspaper, work in cottage industry, binding, polishing, white-washing, collection of waste papers, working in forms, cleaning work in other houses, kniting, sewing and embriodary, helping the parents, and tanning etc. to meet the additional cost of their studies.

9. Major source of loan for meeting the additional cost of study was land owner from higher castes and seek loan from them on interest basis. Sometime they are required to provide security interms of ornaments, for seeking the loan. Other sources of loan were money lenders, rich persons within the caste, relatives, friends and coopertive societies/Bank for meeting the additional cost of their studies.

10. The respondents suggested the updating of educational schemes so as to reduce scheduled castes parents dependence on borrowing and continuance of education of their wards. Most of the teacher were in favour of ancilliary services at primary stage. Only few teachers did not feel the necessity because of their social prejudice. The teachers had suggested the rate of scholarship at different stages according to the latest cost of living.

11. More than half of the teacher were not satisfied with the mode of publicity, and they find that mode of publicity of the schemes are not adequate. The schemes are publicised with short notice. The publicity is also not done in local papers, and even in leading papers, the advertisements are not conspicious. They suggested that the publicity should be made well in advance so that they can perform all formalitles. The local newspapers should be used for publicity. Classified advertisement in new papers specially in bullentians and brochures have also been suggested by the teachers.

12. The teacher considered that the condition of eligibility were heavily biased in favour of privileged

groups within the scheduled castes. They may be re-oriented to cater to the lower section of the scheduled castes by making them more flexible. For example failure of their words is due to cultural deprivation and they are further deprived of the benefit of the schemes as well. They also want relaxation in conditions of eligibility like the revising the income criteria and giving more chance to failed students etc.

13. The scheduled caste face difficulties in the submission of application like indifferent officials, difficult language of the forms and combersome procedure etc. under the educational schemes. The teachers suggested that procedure for submitted application should be simplified. The requirement of completing of formalitis in lengthly forms should be abolished and only minimum essential information should be asked so that every student fill up and submit his application in time.

14. The teachers reported that mode of payment was not satisfactory. The payment are made delayed and the scholarships are misutilised by the some institutions. The teachers suggested streamlining of the disbursemant procedure of payment in periodical instalments and case payment with ampathetic touch of the teacher in disbursement of the amount.

15. In awarding the facilities under different educational schemes, half of the respondents reported that they faced difficulties due to irrational distribution of the facilities. The procedure of the selections are outdated. In additional to this, this is no representation of scheduled castes members in selection committee. They suggested that the representation of a scheduled castes should be invariably involved inselection process for the award of educational facilities. Simple varification can be carried out so the facilities can reach the deserving ones.

16. The teachers also felt that the procedure for renewal of the stripened and scholarships was cumbersome and difficult. The renewal should be automatic.

17. The teachers reported that there are instances where students are eligible for specific schemes but they do not avail of them for certain reasons. The minimum number of the teachers for grade XI have reported non availing of the schemes by the eleigible students. They expressed that some of the economically viable families do not avail of these facilities volunatarily. Some parents are repulsed by the harsh behaviour of the teachers. Another disturbing reasons reporting by the teachers refers to the fear complex in the scheduled castes. They feel that their children will be discriminating socially if their identify is disclosed. The teachers suggested that efforts should be made to educated the massese to overcome the problem of social discrimination and to develop sympathy in teachers towards the disadvantaged groups.

18. The respondents reported the highest drop out potential in grade I and II despite availing of the educational schemes by the children belonging to scheduled caste. It decreases one proceeds onwards. Most of the teacher feel that the students drop out because of sharing responsibility of work with parents. Other major causes of drop-out of the children referes to carelessness of the parents, prolonged absence from the class, and taking care of younger childred at home or illness etc. The respondents suggested that non-formal channel can be used for their education. Congenial environment should be created in school. Advocacy programmes should be launched through the use of media and personal contact.

19. More than half of the respondent felt that the level of acheivement among the scheduled castes was lower in comparison to other castes. Only very few

reported that the achievement level of the scheduled castes is higher than the non-scheduled castes. The respondents expressed various reasons for low achievements. About three fourth of the respondents expressed that children belonging to scheduled castes do not work as hard as other students do. Lack of confidence, lack of concern in parents, lack of initiative, uncongenial environment at home, had habits like drinking and gambling, and low initial cognitive level etc., were the reasons reported by the teachers for a low level of achievement among the scheduled castes. For increasing their achievement level, the first step they suggested refers to the consentization of porents by way of motivation and making them aware of needs for education in view of the complexities of life merging from the changing society. The other suggestion made by the teachers are directed towards their own action, i.e. use of lively methods of teaching involving these situation in classroom transcation accompanied by guidance and counselling programmes for under achievement level. These programmes will be helpful in improving their achievement level. They are to be backed by remedial coaching. The curriculum and textbooks need to be made relevant to the cultural millice of this group of students. Malnutrition is yet another aspects considered to be influencing cognitive and psychomotor of the children. Supplementing nutrition through mid-day meals could help in area. All the factors put together will contribute to the achievement level of the students.

This chapter provided the excursion experiences into the perception of the teachers about education of scheduled castes children in the context of educational schemes floated by Central Government. They have pointed out the difficulties faced by the parents and children in utilisation of educational schemes. They also pointed out the low level of educational achievement among the scheduled castes children having heavy drop outs. Even educational schemes have not been able to hold back the beneficiaries. The major reason is the cognitive lag with which they start due to social disadvantages and isolation in classroom transcation. The organisation aspect of the educational schemes and attitude of the implementors will have to undergo a great change if the schemes have to achieve effectiveness. Teachers can play a vital role in this respects.

14

Attitude of Scheduled Caste Teacher-Trainees Towards Games and Sports

The importance of health and pysical education can hardly be exaggerated in the school curriculum. It is an established fact that provision of this type of education contributes significantly to the development of child's personality. But only those teachers can exploit the potentialities of this curriculum area for pupil development, who have faith in its utility. An individuls faith in a thing obviously depends on his attitude towards that thing. Therefore it is an in the fitness of things if attitude of teachers towards games & sports is ascertained so that appropriate measures are taken to make their attitude positive towards games. The present study was designed with this very end in view.

Objectives

It is a matter of common observation that all the scheduled caste teacher trainees do not form a homogeneous group. They differ from each other with regard to sex, place of living, socio-economic background, educational background etc. As stated above, the main aim of the present investigation is to ascertain which groups of teacher trainees have positive attitudes towards games and sports than the others.

More specifically the objectives of the study can be listed as under :

(i) To ascertain whether men and women belonging to scheduled caste differ from each other significantly in attitudes towards games and sports.

(ii) To determine whether parental occupation has some sort of linkage with attitudes towards games and sports.

(iii) To ascertain whether trainees with subjects differ significantly from other trainees with regard to attitudes towards games and sports.

(iv) To ascertain whether trainees coming from rural areas differ significantly in attitudes towards games and sports from the trainees belonging to urban areas.

(v) To determine the relationship between attitude towards games and sports, and age of the scheduled caste trainees.

(vi) To determine whether previous teacher training is linked with attitudes towards games and sports.

(vii) To determine the relationship between attitude towards games and sports, and performance of the trainees in the qualifying examination.

Sample

The sample of the study comprised of 140 scheduled caste teacher trainees drawn from the colleges of education in Haryana.

Collection of Data

Mr. Yadav's Attitude scale (1976) was selected to measure attitude towards games and sports in the sample population. The scale comprises 20 items, each of which admit five alternative responses. The scale has proved to be reliable and valid tool for the measurement of attitude of teacher trainees towards games and sports. The scale was administered to scheduled caste teacher trainees in the colleges of Haryana in sizeable graups. Proper conditions for the administration of such tests were fully taken care of.

Statistical Analysis

In the first instance, it was decided to explore the possibility of differences in mean scores on the attitude scale towards games and sports in respect of different categories of teacher trainees. The "t" test was employed to test the significance of differences between means. Pearson product-moment coefficient of correlation was computed in order to ascertain the relationship of attitude towards grames and sports of trainees with previous academic achievement and age of the trainees.

Table 14.1 depicts comparative position of different categories of scheduled caste teacher trainees in means performance on attitude scale. Product moment coefficients of correlation between attitude towards games and sports, age and academic achievement scores are given in Table 14.2.

Results and Discussions

1. Teacher trainees whose mothers are working ladies have more positive attitude towards games and sports as compared to the trainees whose mothers are only housewives. This finding is obviously alongwith expected lines. The children of working mothers know the outcome from the game for the bright future from the beginning of their lives. Therefore they have such type of attitude towards games and sports. However, this finding needs further support from more research studies as the number of working monther's included in the sample of the present study is very small.

Table 14.1

Significance of Differences in Mean Scores on Attitude Scale

Categories	(i) *N*	*Mean*	*S.D*	*N*	*Mean*	(ii) *S.D*	*D Mean*	*SED*	*E*
A. *Mother's Occupation* (i) Service (ii) Housewife.	14	41.2	4.4.	126	39.02	6.5	2 18	.52	4.19**
B. *Father's Occupation* (i) Service (ii) Agriculture	4[illegible]	38.9	6.5	64	38.17	6.0	.8	1.9094	.6737
(i) Service (ii) Business	48	38.9	6.5	48	42.35	5.45	3.45	1.4786	2.333*
(i) Business (ii) Agriculture	28	42.35	5.45	64	38.17	6.0	4 18	1.3233	3.1586*
C. *Subjects*									
(i) Arts (ii) Science	97	39.9	6.35	43	36.7	5.5	3.2	1.1182	2.8615*
D. *Place of Living*									
(i) Rural (ii) Urban	84	38.9	6.6	56	39.1	5.5	1.2	1.067	.1871

E. *Sex*									
(i) Male (ii) Female	77	37 909	6.0	63	40 5	6 5	2 591	1.0576	2.449*
F. *Previous Training*									
(i) Fresh (ii) Trained	125	39.1	6 0	15	38.0	6.1	1 1	1 6	0.68

* Significant at .05 level, ** significants at .01 level.

Table 14.2

Significance of Product Moment Coefficients of Correlation

S. No.	*Variable*	*r*	*at*	*Significance level*
1.	Attitude towards games & sports and age of the tranineces	- .07	138	n s.
2.	Teacher attitude towards games & sports and academic achievement	—.011	138	n.s.

2. Table 14.1 reveals that the teacher trainees whose fathers are in service do not differ significantly from the trainees whose fathers are agriculturists, in attitude towards games and sports. This may be due to cost of various games. Teacher trainees whose fathers are in service have negative attitude towards games and businessmen. This findings is on expected lines because these days games are very costly. A businessman's child can afford in comparison to service people. Same is the case with business and agriculture occupation. The trainees whose fathers are agriculturalists have negative attitude in comparison to the trainees whose fathers are businessmen. It may be due to the cost of games. Therefore they differ significantly in attitude towards games and sports.
3. Table 14.1 reveals that trainees with science subjects differ significantly in attitude towards games and sports from the trainees with other subjects. This result is also alongwith the expected lines because science students have no time to take part in games. They are required to work for longer hours in their institution and laboratories.
4. The study has revealed that attitude towards games and sports has got no linkage with place of livings. This implies that the trainees belonging to rural areas do not have more positive or negative attitude towards games and sports than the urbanities. Both the groups may have their peculiar problems but the same do not appear to be related to attitude towards games and sports.
5. The study reveals that it is the female trainees who have more positive attitude towads games and sports as compared to male trainees.
6. It is clear from table 14.1 that attitude towards games and sports has got no linkage with previous training. This implies the trainees with previous teacher training do not possess more favourable or

unfavourable attitude towards games and sports than the fresh trainees. However, this finding needs to be further verified because of small number of trained teachers in the sample of the present study.

7. Table 14.2 reveals that the product moment coefficient of correlation between attitude towords games and sports and age of trainees is—.7, which is not significant statistically. Thus it has become clear that no linkage exists between these two variables, that is, age of the trainees has bothing to do with the attitude towards games and sports.
8. It is clear from the table that the product moment coefficient of correlation (r) between attitude towards games and sports, and previous academic achievement is—.011, which is not statistically significant. Thus it has become clear that no linkage exists between these two variables, that is, previous academic achievement has nothing to do with attitud towards games and sports.

Educational Implications

This study has some important implications for teacher education programmes. The scheduled caste trainees having adverse attitude towards games and sports should be located in the beginning of the session, therefore, suitable strategies will have to be adopted to change their attitude towards games and sports because it is very likely to help them to become an effective teacher.

15

Attitude of Teacher Trainees Towards Teaching

All round development of the personality of the child is the aim of education. This objective of education can be realised only when the teaching learning is effective. Effective teaching is the medium through which the development of total personality takes place. Teaching can be said to be effective if the teacher is able to motivate the learness to learn in desired direction. In teaching learning process teacher's attitude play a very important role because they not only affect his behaviour in the classroom but also influence the behaviour of his students. Moreover, effective and productive learning on the part of students can be achieved by selecting teachers with desirable attitude or by shaping their attitudes in the desired direction. For the selectipn of the right types of teachers, measurement of attitude towards teaching profession is essential at the time of selection, for the teacher training. This study is an attempt in this direction.

Objectives

It is a matter of common observation that all the scheduled caste teacher trainees do not form a homogenous group. They differ from each other with regard to sex, place of living, socio-economic background and educational background etc. As stated above, the aim of the present investigation is to ascertain whether different groups of teacher trainees differ in their attitude towards teaching profession.

Hypothesis

Based on the above objectives, the following hypothesis were framed :

1. There is no significant difference between the male and female scheduled caste teachers regarding their attitude towards teaching profession.
2. There is no significant difference between the scheduled caste teacher trainees whose fathers belong to service and agriculture, service and business, business and agricultural occupations, regarding their attitude towards teaching profession.
3. There is no significant difference between the scheduled caste teacher trainees whose mothers belonging to service and household occupations, concerning their attitude towards teaching profession.
4. There is no significant difference between the scheduled caste, teacher trainees belonging to art and science groups concerning their attitude towards teaching profession.
5. There is no significant difference between the means of rural and urban scheduled caste trainees in their attitude towards teaching profession.
6. There is no significant difference between the scheduled caste teacher trainees belonging to fresh and trained group, in their attitude towards teaching profession.
7. There is no relationship between attitude towards teaching profession and age of teacher trainees belonging to scheduled caste.

8. There is no relationship between attitude towards teaching profession and academic achievement of the teacher trainees belonging to scheduled castes.

Methodology

Sample

The sample of the study comprised of 145 scheduled caste Pupil teacher from colleges of Education in Haryana.

Tool Used

Dr. Ahluwalia Teacher attitude inventory was related to measure the attitude of teacher trainees towards teaching profession. The inventory comprises 90 items. Each item has five point scale : i.e. Strongly Agree, Agree, Undecided, Disagree and strongly Disagree. The theoritical range of score is from 0 to 360 with the higher score indicating more favourable attitude towards teaching and allied subjects. The inventory has proved to be a reliable and valied tool for the measurement of attitude towards teaching profession.

Analysis and Treatment of Dat

In the first instance, it was decided to explore the possibility of differences in mean scores on the attitude towards teaching profession in respect of different categories of teacher trainees. The "t-test" was employed to test the significance of differences between means. Pearson's product moment co-efficient of correlation was computed in order to ascertain the relationship of attitude towards teaching profession of trainees with previous academic achievement and age of the trainees.

Table 15.1 depicts comparative position of different categories of scheduled caste teacher trainees in mean performance on attitude scale. Product moment co-efficient of correlation between attitude towards teaching profession, age and academic achievement scores are given in Table 15.2.

Table 15.1
Significance of Differences in Mean Scores on Attitude scale

Categories	*N(I) N*	*Mean*	*S.D.*	*N.*	*(II) Mean*	*S.D. Mean*	*D*	*S.E. D*	*T Value*
1	*2*	*3*	*4*	*5*	*6*	*7*	*8*	*9*	*10*
A. *Sex*									
(i) Male	50	246.38	17.37	95	247.02	24.22	.64	43.120	*0.01482
(ii) Female									
B. *Father's Occupation*									
1. Service	69	246.6	20.65	40	247.55	21.7	9	418	* .2152
2. Agriculture									
1. Service	69	246.6	20.65	36	248.3	24.78	.7	455	*15.38
2. Business									
1. Business	36	247.3	24.78	40	247.5	21.7	.2	5.32	*0 0375
2. Service									
C. *Mother's Occupation*									
1. Service	11	243.0	27.38	133	247.05	21.98	3.97	2.038	*1.9556
2. Housewife									

(Contd.)

1	2	3	4	5	6	7	8	9	10
D. *Subjects*									
Arts	112	228.4	23.10	33	241 5	17.22	6.9	4.342	*1.6046
Science									
E. *Place of Living*									
1. Rural	61	248.91	21 00	84	148.16	22.68	.85	41.7986	*0.012033
2. Urban									
F. *Previous Training*									
1. Fresh	125	248.2	22.30	20	238 05	17.7	10.15	5.2435	*10.937
2. Trained									

* not significant

Results and Discussion

To test the hypothesis at Sr. No (i) to (vi), t-test was employed to find out the significant difference between mean scores or various categories of teacher trainees. The values of t-test were not found to be significant in any category. So all the six hypothesis were retained. It means sex, place of living, parent's occupation, subjects and previous training have no impact on the attitude of teacher trainees towards teaching profession. In case of science and art group, and fresh and trained teachers, there is difference in mean scores but the difference is not significant. Agarwal (1980) also did not find significant difference between male and female teacher trainees in attitude of teachers towards teaching profession. Table 15.2 reveals that the product moment coefficient of correlation between attitude towards teaching profession and age of trainees is —09, which is not significant statistically. Thus it has become clear that no linkage exist between these two variables, i.e. age of the trainees has nothing to do with the attitude towards teaching profession. Therefore, the hypothesis at Sr. No. (VII) is retained. It is also clear from the Table that

Table 15.2

Significance of Product Moment Coefficient of Correlation

	Variable	*N*	*df*	*r*	*Significance level*
1.	Attitude towards teaching profession and age of teacher trainees	145	143	—09	Not significant
2.	Teacher trainees attitude towards teaching profession and academic achievement	145	143	.037	Not significant

the product moment co-efficient of correlation (r) between attitude towards teaching profession and previous academic achievement is 0.037 which is not statistically significant. Therefore, the hypothesis at Sr. No. (VIII) is also retained. It means previous academic achievement has nothing to do with the attitude towards teaching profession.

Education Implications

The study has important educational implications for the selection of the scheduled caste teachers trainees for admission to B.Ed. course. The trainees having positive attitude towards teaching profession should be selected so that they can work for the growth of the teaching profession.

16

Parental and Students Awareness about Educational Schemes

In the early Vedic Period Indian Society was castless in the sense that all types of work was done by each and every body according to their potentialities. Every member of the family was at liberty to adopt any profession he liked best without any reservation. Born of the same parents one son used to tend the cattle and till the soil; the second son having perhaps mercantile bias, carried on trade and commerce, the third one being of an enterprising nature, defended his health and home against aggressors and maintained peace and order in the country; and again the fourth son, gifted with intellectual and spiritual dispositions, pursued the prietly profession (M.H.A : 1975).

This arrangement was possible only in very simple society where population, needs and the resources are extemely limited. With the increased population and growing complexity of Vedic Aryans in course of time, the concept of qualities (gunas) and action (Karma) was injected into the social system in form of chaturvana "Four Castes"—Brahmana, Kshatriya, Vaishya and Shudra by Shri Krishna of the upanishadic age (BC.C. 1956). To start with, the system in Vedic times worked very well, because there was no discrimination on the basis of the occupation, all men were equal, there was no trace of untouchability, no man was considered too high and no man too low as envisaged in the Rig Veda, every member of community ate and drink with others and envisaged in the Atharva Veda, the community was bound by a feeling of brotherhood and the earth was treated as the mother and everyone cooperated in the welfare of the community.

But, with the passage of time, the system degenerated into caste rigidities and the shudras were pushed to the lowest rung of the caste hireracby, so much so a time came when they become untouchable. After sometime sudras were called Depressed class also and the term "Scheduled Caste" appeared for the first time in the Govt. of India Act, 1935. In April 1936, specifying certain castes, races and tribes as scheduled castes in the then provinces of Assam, Bengal, Bihar, Bombay, Central Provinces & Berar, Madras, Orissa, Punjab and United Provinces. The dawn in 1950 was a revised version of the list of Scheduled Castes under the Govt. of India (Scheduled Castes) order 1936. (M.H.A. 1975). After pushing Sudras in lowest rung, the avenues of education and socio-economic availability were completely closed for them. As a consequence people belonging to these castes faced socio-economic insecurity and remained backward and illiterates since ages due to several reasons.

Keeping in view the above, several efforts were made to improve the conditions of scheduled castes prior to independance and post-independance. A special provision was made for the first time in the central budget in 1944 for the grant of scholarship for education of backward communities including scheduled castes and special facilities have been provided for them in free India.

The authors of the Constitution of India envisage ample safeguards for the scheduled castes. Article 46 of the constitution states; "The state shall promote with special care the educational and economic interests of the weaker sections of the people and shall protect them from social injustice and all forms of exploitation". To implement the enshrined in the constitution. Policy regarding scheduled castes the Government of India have made liberal allocation of funds for their amelioration in the National Five Year plans i.e. 9.28 crores, 11.89 crores, 40.00 crores, 66 crores 220 crores and 960.30 crores during first, second, third and fourth, fifth and sixth plans respectively. It has been allocated for more in seventh five year plan.

The Central Govt. and most of the State Govts. have meaningful programmes and schemes for their betterment. Some of these are as follows :

(i) Pre-matric scholarships and incentives like free supply of books, stationery, dress, mid-day meals etc.

(ii) Post matric scholarships;

(iii) Technical Education;

(iv) Overseas scholarships;

(v) Hotels and Hostel facilities;

(vi) Ashram schools and Residential Schools;

(vii) Special incentives for girls education;

(viii) Reservation for scheduled caste children in Sainik school, I.T.I.'s and other educational Institutions;

(ix) Coaching and Vocational guidance at various levels.

Despite efforts by the Union and the States Govts, for encouraging their education, the progress of scheduled caste is poor and there is wide gap in the literacy rate as well as in the enrolment between scheduled caste and non-scheduled Goyal, (1981) also pointed out the prevalence of disprity between the scheduled castes and general castes. The wide gap in literacy and enrolment of both groups of scheduled caste and other communities indicate that the efforts made so far are far from satisfactory. In order to improve the situation, it is desirable that scientific studies may be made into the causes of the unsatisfactory progress and plan suitable programmes for the same. This study is an effort in this direction.

The investigator, threfore, proposes to study awareness amongst the scheduled castes about the schemes for their educational progress an its implications for educational planning. This particular study has been designed, since emperical work in this area is conspicuous by its absence.

The slow progress in the education of the scheduled castes as reflected in low enrolment ratio and literacy rate despite various efforts of the government, for accelerating the pace of their educational progress, raises several pertinent questions. Are the scheduled castes aware of the facilities provided by the government under different schemes? If not, why? If yes, are they utilising these facilities properly? If they are not utilising the facilities properly, is there something wrong with the schemes themselves or are they precluded by some other causes? What can be done to improve the functional effectiveness of the scheme? Objective assessment of the existing position based on scientifically collected data are essential for securing answers to the questions posed above. It is further desirable to study the problem in the context of a limited area. The Union Territory of Delhi where educational facilities are more can provide a viable area for study. It is for this purpose, the present study was planned.

The Problem

The specific problem can be stated as "A study of the Scheduled Caste's Awareness About the Schemes for Their Educational Progress".

Definition of Terms

In this study, the following concepts are used :

(I) Awareness

(II) Scheduled Caste

(I) Awareness

Such information about schemes which would enable to the people or their parents to know that they can be benefited by the schemes.

(II) Scheduled Caste

"Scheduled Castes" according to the Constitution of India means such castes, races or tribes or parts of groups within such castes, races or tribes as deemed under article 341 of the Constitution of India to be scheduled castes.

Objectives

The specific objectives of the study can be stated as under :

1. To identify the educational schemes for facilitating education of the children belonging to scheduled castes.
2. To study the awareness of students and heads of family regarding the educational schemes for facilitating education of the children.
3. To study the sources of awareness about the educational schemes for facilitating education of children belonging to scheduled castes.
4. To study the antecedent variables of the awareness level of the heads of family regarding the educational schemes for facilitating education of the children belonging to scheduled castes.
5. To study the relationship between the awareness of heads of family about educational schemes and their utilisation by children belonging to scheduled castes.
6. To study the relationship between the awareness of heads of family about educational schemes and the drop-out rate of children belonging to scheduled castes.

7. To study the relationship between the awareness of scheduled caste's heads of family about educational schemese and their attending children.
8. To study the relationship between awareness of scheduled castes heads of family about educational schemes and their non-attending children.
9. To study the relationship between awareness of scheduled castes heads of family about educational schemes and their out-of-school children.
10. To study the problems faced by the scheduled castes in the utilisation of educational schemes for facilitating education of their children.
11. To identify the directions for procedural modification with a view to facilitating utilisation of the educational schemes by the children belon-ing to scheduled castes with particular reference to the conditions of eligibility, value of scholarships, awards of schemes, duration and renewal of awards, mode of payment, mode of publicity and submitting application.

Hypothesis

In order to realise the objectives of the study outlined above, the following null hypothesis were formulated :

Ho 1. There is no significatnt difference in the awareness of educational schemes among urban, semi-urban and rural heads of family belonging to scheduled castes.

Ho 2. There is no significant difference in the awareness of educational schemes among urban, semi-urban and rural students belonging to scheduled castes.

Ho 3. There is no significant difference in the awareness of educational schemes among urban, semi-urban and rural male students belonging to scheduled castes.

Ho 4. There is no significant difference in the awareness of educational schemes among urban, semi-urban and rural female students belonging to scheduled castes.

Ho 5. There is no significant difference in the awareness of educational schemes between male and female students belonging to scheduled castes

Ho 6. Awareness of the heads of family about educational schemes and the caste within scheduled castes to which they belong are independent of each other.

Ho 7. Awareness of students about educational schemes and the caste within scheduled castes to which they belong are independent to each other.

Ho 8. Awareness of heads of family and students about schemes for their educational progress belonging to scheduled castes are not significantly related.

Ho 9. There is no significant difference in the yearly income of the heads of family in rural, semi-urban and urban areas.

Ho 10. There is no significant difference in the per capita income of the families belonging to scheduled castes in rural, semi-urban and urban areas.

Ho 11. Awareness of heads of family about educational schemes and yearly income of the families belonging to scheduled castes are not significantly related.

Ho 12. Awareness of heads of family about educational schemes and per capita income of the families belonging to scheduled caste are not significantly related.

Ho 13. The educational level of the heads of family and locations they belong to are independent of each other.

Ho 14. Awareness of heads of family about educational schemes and educational level of the heads of family belonging to scheduled castes are independent of each other.

Ho 15. The occupational level of the scheduled caste heads of family and the location areas are independent of each other.

Ho 16. Awareness of head of the family about educational schemes and their occupational level are independent of each other.

Ho 17. Awareness of the heads of the family about the educational schemes and the utilisation of educational schemes by their wards are independent of each other.

Ho 18. Awarenese of heads of family about educational schemes and attending children are independent of each other.

Ho 19. Awareness of heads of family about educational schemes and drop-out rate of children are independent of each other.

Ho 20. Awareness of heads of family about educational schemes and non-attending children are independent of each other.

Ho 21. Awareness of heads of family about educational schemes and rate of out of school children are independent of each other.

Procedure

Population in the case of the present study has defined as people belonging to scheduled castes, the Union Territory of Delhi. The unit of the sample was family. One hundred families from selected rural, semi-urban and urban areas of Delhi were covered. At the first stages of selection of locations, the locations having concentration of scheduled caste population were selected. From these locations, families were selected randomly.

Two questionnaires and an Awareness Level Scoring Key (ALSK) were developed for the collection of data for the study. The first questionnaire purported to collect information from scheduled caste heads of family and the second one from the students. An awareness level scoring key was meant for assessing awareness of both heads of family and the students.

The data were collected during field work through administering the questionnaires to the heads of the families and students covered in the study. The investigator filled in the questionnaires through interview from the illiterate heads of the family and from those who were literate upto primary stage. The questionnaires of students were filled in by the investigator through interview at the primary stage and beyond primary stage questionnaires were filled in by the students themselves.

In order to test the hypothesis relating to awareness, T-test, chisquare and product moment co-efficient of correlation were computed. To analyse data regarding problems and suggestions, the percentage were calculated.

Findings

The significant findings emerging from the study are given below.

Source of Awareness

School is the major source of awareness of the heads of the family about educational schemes, since more than fifty per cent respondent have indicated this source. Only a quarter of them consider newspaper as the source, while a few consider neighbour's children, the notice board in schools and colleges, teachers, friends and relatives to be the sources of their awareness.

Antecedent of Awareness

1. The awareness level of heads of the family tends to differ in different, location areas. The urban heads of femily have higher level of awareness about educational schemes than heads of the family in semi-urban and rural areas.
2. The trend in the awareness level of students about the education scheme follows the trend in the awareness level of heads of the family. The students in the urban areas have higher awareness than those in semi-urban and rural areas.

3. When viewed sex-wise, awareness level of the urban male students is higher than that of the rural male students. The differences, however, were singnificant between urban and rural students on awareness about schemes only.
4. Awareness level of the urban female students is significantly higher than that of the rural female students. The awareness level of the semi-urban female student was also significantly higher than that of rural female students; while the differences between the awareness level of the urban and semi-urban female student is not found to be significant.
5. Taking the total sample of students, awareness level of male students is found to be higher than that of the female students. The result holds good in the three location areas as well.
6. There is association between castes within scheduled castes and awareness level of the heads of family irrespective of location areas to which they belong.
7. There is association between the castes within scheduled castes and awareness level of the student irrespective of the location areas. This shows congruence between the awareness level of heads of family and student on this variable.
8. The congruence between the awareness level of heads of family and students is further corroborated by the significant 'r' values.
9. The yearly income of the head of family differ in different location areas, namely, rural, semi-urban and urban. Urban heads of family having higher income level than that of semi-urban heads of family and semi-urban heads of family having higher income than that of the rural heads of family. The same trend holds good in case of per capita income of the families except in case of rural and semi-urban areas, where the difference in the per capita incomes of families was not found significant between them.

10. There is positive significant relationship between the income of heads of family and his awareness level. In the differentitated results, however, the relationships is positive but not significant in the case of rural heads of family. The same trend features in the per capita income of the family and awareness of head of family.

11. The educational level of the heads of family belonging to scheduled castes has association with location areas, namely rural, semi-urban and urban areas. This implies that their educational level varies from area to area.

12. Awareness of heads of family is associated with their educational level in the total sample when viewed differentially according to location areas, the awareness of heads of family is not related to their educational level in rural area, while the relationship between the two variables exists in urban and semi-urban areas.

13. The occupational level of the heads of family has association with location areas, namely rural, semi-urban and urban areas.

14. There is relationship between the awareness level of heads of family and their occupation in the total sample irrespective that the two variables are not related in rural and semi-urban areas.

Consequences of Awareness

15. There is association between awareness of scheduled caste heads of family and utilisation of the educational schemes by their wards as revealed by significant chi-square values. The result holds in rural, semi-urban and urban areas. Higher the awareness level of the heads of family, the higher is the incidence of attending children.

16. The awareness level of heads of family about schemes has an association with the drop-out rate of children. The result holds good for the three location areas—rural, semi-urban and urban. The higher the awareness level, lower is the drop out rate.

17. The awareness level of scheduled caste heads of family about schemes for their educational progress is found to be significantly associated with the out-of-school children (non-attending+drop out). The results are consistent in the three location areas as well.

Problems and Suggestions

18. More than one half of the heads of family feel that the educational schemes are partly significant to meet the educational costs, while some (17.0 per cent) heads of family are of the opinion that the existing schemes are sufficient to meet the expenses of their children's education. About one fourth of the heads of family consider that the educational schemes provided by the government for the welfare of scheduled castes are insufficient.

19. The heads of family suggested that rate of scholarship should be increased. Ancillary services and uniforms should be given to all students belonging to scheduled castes. They also feel that residential hostels should be provided to their wards for providing conducive environment for education which is absent at their houses.

20. The heads of family find the publicity of educational schemes as inadequate. They want timely publicity to be made more effective by using multi-media approach.

21. The heads of family have pointed to the social prejudices as reflected by the use of derogatory language for those availaing the facilities. This, they think, should be remodified through educating public opinion an the issue.

22. The heads of the family cansider the condition of eligibility heavily biased in favour of privilaged groups within scheduled castes. They may be reoriented to cater to the lowest section of scheduled castes by making them more flexible. For example failure of their wards is due to cultural deprivation and they are further deprived of the benefits of schemes as well. They also want relaxation in conditions of aligibility like raising the means level and requirement of documents.
23. The independent and corrupt officers responsible for the implementation are also considered road-blocks in the way of effective utilisation of the educational schemes. Careful selection and effective supervision have been suggested as measures to tackle the problem.
24. The heads of family consider the difficulties at the time of receiving payment like irrational distribution, inefficient officials, indifferent attitude of officials, cumbersome procedure, mode of payment and delayed payment. They have given suggestions to remove the difficulties through prompt payment, rational distribution, direct release of grants, legal guardianship, fixed date and time, payment in full and cash and sympathetic attitude of the officials.
25. The heads of family consider the precedure for the renewal of schemes as cumbersome and unnecessary. The renewal should be automatic.

Implications

The relationship between awareness level of the heads of family about educational schemes for their wards and the consequent variables of utilisation level of educational schemes, rate of attending, drop-rate, and of non-attending and out-of school children have provided significant findings. The utilisation level of the educational shemes has been found to be associated with the level of awareness of head of family. Same is the case with other variables.

Awareness of the heads of family has emerged as potential and desirable variable. An examination of its antecedent variables indicate the direction for developing the awareness. Educational, Economic and occupational level of the heads of family have found to be associated with the awareness level of heads of family, which implies that the raising of educational, occupational and economic level of heads of family is likely to increase their awareness level. For raising the educational level of heads of family through programmes of adult aducation, non-formal education and continuing education can go a long way in accelerating the process of improving their awareness level. Social emphasis, therefore, is called for this section of Indian society which has been neglected for a long time.

The parents also reported the various procedural difficulties in availing the schemes, so the evaluation of each of the educational schemes in terms of the specific objective should be done on emperical basis.

The heads of family pointed out that attitude of officers for implementing the schemes is indifferent and unsymphthetic. Therefore, these officers and staff members should be provided training in human relations.

Conclusion

Awareness of heads of family has emerged as a meaningful variable for study in the context of educational schemes for the progress of scheduled caste children. The study of antecedents and consequent variables of awareness has provided direction for improving the awareness level of heads of family so as to increase their utilisation and increase the incidence of the education amongst scheduled castes. A lot has been done in this direction and a lot more needs to be done. It is hoped that the findings and implications of the study summarised above will be helpful be those concerned with planning and implementation of the schemes to usher in era of educational progress for the long neglected section of the Indian society.

17

Research Perspective

The preceding chapters outlined the context specified plans and procedures of the book. The National policy perspective, the research reviews and research studies on scheduled castes have been highlighted. This chapter purports to focus research perspective and its implications for action. Obviously, the research perspective has been derived from the findings of the studies reported earlier in this beak. The present chapter includes guidelines for different government and voluntary agencies and institutions concerned with the progress of scheduled castes, NPE—1986 has also laid stress on research and micro studies.

It has been observed from the research reviews covered under section—A that the scheduled caste people are still suffering from the evils like untouchability in some parts of the country. No doubt the extent of untouchability has decreased in some parts of the country due to the efforts made by the government and other agancies. This area requires more research attention so that the problems can be brought to the notice of the government. The rate of wastage and also found more among scheduled caste non-scheduled caste students. The reviews also highlight the awareness level of the partners about educational schemes and their utilisation level. Various constraints and road blocks for utilisation of educational schemes and their action points for their solutions have also been discussed in overview of researches. Some psychological studies on motivational aspects, intelligence, academic achievement, adjustment, attitude self-concept and aspiration level among scheduled castes have been reviewed which showed the discouraging results as compared to general caste people.

The research studies under section—B revealed some disturbing findings which require attention by the government and voluntary agencies for the betterment of scheduled caste people. The demographic profile study showed that the income per capita level of the scheduled caste families was much lower than national percapital level. The average family size of the scheduled caste was 9.8 which was almost one and half times more than the national average size of 6.2. They are mostly unskilled labour and working in unclean occupation. The picture regarding their educational status is very dismal. The literacy rate, according to 1981 census, among scheduled castes was much lower as compared to general caste. Mostly parents are illiterate and majority of their children hardly cross the primary classes and the dropout rate is very high. The study of motivation and intellectual level among scheduled caste and non-scheduled caste secondary students showed no significant difference on intelligence level between the two and the motivational tendencies showed the mixed result. When the vacational anxiety was studied it was found more among the scheduled caste teacher trainees as compared to non-scheduled caste trainees. They were feeling more insecure and anxious. It has been found that there is more insecurity concerning participation in vocations among female scheduled caste children.

Another investigation on teacher perception about educational schemes for the education of scheduled castes had revealed that most of the children were availing the educational schemes. They would find it difficult to continue there education without these benefits and schemes. The teachers also stated that the young children are engaged in tea stalls and factories for supplementing the income of their families which deprives them from getting education. The scheduled caste parents have to seek loan from their relatives and friends for meeting the expenses of their children studies because the existing rate of scholarship is not sufficient to meet the cost of education. Besides the existing procedure for publishing these schemes, submission of application, distribution and renewal procedure of these schemes was found faulty and lengthey. The teachers reported that the academic achievement of the scheduled caste was much lower as compared to their counter parts. It requires research attention in depth for rationalising the system.

The attitude of teacher trainees towards games and sports was found positive in general but it varied in different categories. The teacher trainees whose mothers are in jobs have more positive attitude than those whose mothers are housewives. But the trainees whose fathers are in service have negative attitude towards games and sports as compared to those trainees whose fathers are in business. Since students differ in attitude from the arts students and the female students have positive attitude than the male students. It also revealed that attitude towards games and sports has no association with place of their livings and their previous training.

Regarding the attitude of teacher trainees towards teaching, no significant difference was found on the means scores of their sex, place of living, parents, occupation, subjects and previous training. In case of science and art group; and fresh and trained teachers there is difference in mean scores but it is not significant. Age and previous academic achivement of the trainees has no linkage with their attitude towards teaching.

The awareness study of parents and their children about educational schemes revealed that urban parents and their children had more awareness about educational schemes than rural counterparts. The males were found more aware than females. The awareness also varied within the scheduled castes. Awareness level has positive relationship with place of living, occupation, income and education level. Awareness increases the utilisation level of the educational schemes. The aware parents and students utilise more schemes as compared to unaware parents and their children. The educational level of the children of the aware parents was found to be higher as compared to children of unaware parents. The awareness level of heads of family about schemes has also an association with the dropout children. This holds good for rural and urban areas. The higher the awareness level, lower is the drop-out rate. This holds true in case of non-attending and out of school children.

From the research overviews and research studies on scheduled caste, it has become evident that the emphasis has been on historical, comparative and survey type researchers. These type of researches, no doubt, bring fruitful results but leave some gaps. Mostly studies have been conducted by surveying social, educational and occupational aspects which donot fulfil the desired goal. Very few studies have been conducted by adopting an experimental design. This type of researches certainly pinpoint the problems and will help in ameliorating the conditions of scheduled castes. Besides this for better action research and psychological research by following experimental design should be conducted not only in some areas but all aspects of education for the total development of the children belonging to scheduled castes. Innovative techniques and methodology should be employed. In this regard, some of the areas for the research are suggested below :

—National curriculum
—Language development
—Women education
—Education for disabled
—Early childhood education
—Non-formal education
—National integration
—Navodaya Vidalay
—Vocationalisation of education

—Computer literacy
—Cultural perspective
—Value-oriented education
—Educational technology
—Work experience
—Teacher education
—Environmental education
—Science education
—Examination reform
—Continuing education
—Teaching learning strategies
—Nutrition and health education
—Parent education
—Population education
—Art education
—Higher education
—Technical and management education
—Media and educational technology
—Management of education

Experimental research using innovative techniques like mastery learning should be conducted in the above mentioned areas for the development of the scheduled castes. An experimental study entilted 'Effect of Mastery Learning Strategris on Cogintive and Non-cognitive' Attainment of scheduled caste students in Science and Mathematics on sample basis is given in discussed the annexure for generating new projects in the area of education for scheduled castes.

In conclusion, this chapter has discussed the major findings of defferent research studies conducted in the light of recent trends and the gaps between the researches have been pinpointed. Experiment and action researches studis have suggested for better results. In this regard a sample study of experimental design has been discussed for the total development of the scheduled caste people. Such researches on scheduled caste will certainly help in minimising the gaps and dispareties between the so called lower and higher caste people.

Annexure

A Sample Study

Effect of Mastery Learning Strategies on Cognitive and Non-cognitive Attainment of Scheduled Castes Students in Science and Mathematics.

The Context

According to 1981 Census the population Scheduled was 10.4 crores which is about 16 per cent to the total population. Milllions of their children go to school for their reducation. They spend 40 to 45 hours per week for ten to twelve years in the process. The Central and State Government also provided special facilities and schemes for their education. This is huge investment in terms of time as well as money. Despite all these efforts in the education of children, pupils achievement leaves much to be desired.

Children are believed to be normally distributed with respect to their cognitive and non-cognitive attributes like intelligence, attitude, attitude and other personality traits. Similarly it is also believed that pupil's are normally distributed with respect to their achievement in the field of learning. This way in the present system of education, academic goals for teachers and students appear to be pre-determined. It reduces teacher's aspiration and pupils desires for further learning. Further it systematically destroys the ego and self concept of a sizeable proportion of students who are legally required to attend school for eight years under conditions which are systematically frustrating and humiliating. It results in development of negative self concept and attitude in child life. This results into stagnation and ultimate dropout. Besides, it exposes the system to enormous wastage of resources. A matter of concern to all connected with education indeed.

The logical question arising out of what has been stated above is as to whether this should be allowed to drift along or should a way be found out to find a solution of the problem. If so, how could it be possible? Carroll's Model of School Learning (1963) and Blooms concept of Mastery Learning (1968, 1976) provides a sound basis for optimising pupil's learning in different curricula areas.

Mastery learning envisages that it is possible to help 90-95 per cent of the learners to acquire 90-95 per cent of the content taught through the use of appropriate material and increasing time for learning for the pupils falling shory of the desired mastery level. Few steps in the mastery learning summarised by Jangira (1980) are :

Step-I : Development of sequentional teaching units are prepared on the content to be taught. Units tests are also developed alongwith teaching units. These teste aim at measuring the mastery level of the pupils and provide feed-back to both teachers and pupils for further instruction to be provided to the pupils falling short. These tests of the mastery level are administered after completion of each teaching unit.

Deciding the Mastery Level

Step-II : The mastery levels are decided. This may indicate the percentage of children learning, the percentage of content taught to the pupils. The desired mastery level ranges from 85 per cent to 100 per cent learning by students.

Teaching the Units

Step-III : The units is taught to the class as a whole in a was that maximum number of pupils learn mavimum of the content taughts.

Assessing Mastery Level

Step-IV : Mastery test is administered immediately after the completion of the first unit. This test will show the extent of pupils learning. This information may be used to identify the pupils who have learnt at the desired mastery. They may be grouped together (A). Such pupils who do not come to the desired level need little more help to come up to the desire a level may be grouped as (B) and students who have remained for behind the decided level may be grouped as (C).

Making Renewed Effortrs

Step-V : The pupils in groups (B) and (C) are again taught using modified teaching approach. Small group instruc tion, peer instruction and pair instruction can be utilised for the purpose. Selected students from group (A) can be engaged in supervising and helping group (B). Teacher may reteach group (C) by modified approach keeping in view the difficulties of children.

Step-VI : Pupils in groups (B) and (C) are given Mastery test. The pupils achieveing the decided level will join group (A).

Organizing Tutrisals

Step-VII : For the remaining children who have failed to achieve the desired level of learning will be provided tutorials by the teacher and selected students from group (A) as per need. Pupils individual difficulties will be searched out at this stage and will be solved accordingly.

Teaching the Next Unit

Step-VIII : Step-I to VII be repeated and desired level

of learning will be achieved for this unit as well and similarly all the units will be completed.

Several studies have been conducted a broad to find out the effectiveness of Mastery Learning strategy related to different curricula areas for different grades. (Kim Hogwon et. al. 1969, Karsh, 1970). Reviewing these studies, Bloom, (1978), concludes that it is possible to improve mastery level of pupils different subjects areas through the strategy of Mastery Learning approach. A few studies being conducted in India with general pupils have revealed encourageing results (Yadav, 1981, Mathur. 1981). It is also observed that pupils also improve their self-concept as well as they develop positive attitudes towards the subject taught. As a corrollary, if the technique is used with pupils from scheduled castes and other weaker sections, their interest in school will be increased. They are likely to continue their study due to decreased drop-out. Moreover, the quality of attainment of the pupils who are not potential dropout is also likely to improve. It is, therefore, desirable to study if the Mastery Learning Strategy which is diffective with general students can also be effective in improving attainments of scheduled caste children. If so, it will provide a break through in optimising instructional effectiveness of these children. Empirical study can provide answer to this question. The present study is an attempt in this direction.

Statement of the Problems

The Problem for the present study can be stated as :

Effect of Mastery Learning Strageties on Cognitive and Non-cognitive Attainment of Scheduled Castes Students in science and Mathematics.

It is evident from the title that the method of teaching "Mastery Learning Strategy" versus conventional method of teaching Mathematics and Science constitute the independent variable, pupils cognitive and non-cognitive attainment constitute the dependent variables. Mathematics and Science have been selected for the simple reason that achievement of pupils in this area in India has been found to be much lower than that of other countries (Husen; 1967). This is particulary so in pupils for weaker sections. Two independent variables have been selected from the affective domain because the level of achievement has been found to be related to the level achievement (Bloom, 1971). The pupil achievement is proposed to be adjusted on intelligence and their socio-economic status.

Objective of the Study

The specific objective of the study can be stated as below :

1. To study the effect of Mastery Learning Strategy on the achievement of 6th grade scheduled caste pupil's in Mathematics;
2. To study the effect of Mastery Learning Strategy on the achivement of 6th grade scheduled caste pupils in Science.
3. To study the effect of Mastery Learning Strategy on pupil's self concept in Science and Mathematics teaching;
4. To study the effect of Mastery Learning Strategy of pupil s adjustment in Science and Mathematics teaching; and
5. To study the effect of Mastery Learning Strategy on pupil's attitude towards Science and Mathematics teaching.

Fypothesis

To realise the objectives of the study, the following null hypothesis have been formulated :

First Type

1. At the end of their experiment the scheduled caste pupils taught with M.L.S. scores significantly higher on Mathematics achievement test than the group of scheduled caste pupil's taught without M.L.S.,

2. At the end of their experiment the scheduled caste pupil taught with M.L.S. score significantly higher on Science Achievement test than the group of scheduled caste pupils taught without M.L.S.,
3. At the end of their experiment the scheduled caste pupils taught with M.L.S. scores reveal significantly higher level of positive self-concept than the group of scheduled caste pupils taught without M.L S.,
4. At the end of thier experiment the scheduled caste pupils taught with M.L.S. score significantly higher on adjustment test than the group of scheduled caste pupils taught without M.L.S., and
5. At the end of their experiment the scheduled caste pupils taught with M.L.S. scores significantly higher on attitude scale than the group of scheduled caste pupils taught without M.L.S.

Second Type

1. The scheduled caste pupils taught using M.L S. show significant gains in Mathematics achievement scores than the pupils taught without M.L.S.,
2. The scheduled caste pupils taught uging M.L.S. show significantly against in Science achievement scores than the pupils taught without M.L.S.,
3. The scheduled caste pupils taught using M.L.S. show significantly gains in self-concept scores than the pupils taught without M.L.S.,
4. The scheduled caste pupils taught using M.L.S. show significantly gains in adjustment scores than the pupils taught without M.L.S., and
5. The scheduled caste popils taught using M.L.S. show significantly gains in attitude scores then the pupils taught without M.L.S.

Design

The study employs Pre-test, Post-test and control group designs. It involves two groups of scheduled caste students-one experimental and the other control group. The study will be carried in three stages, first stage involves testing of cognitive and non-cognitive aspects of the personality of scheduled caste students i.e. their intelligence, socio-economic status, achievement, self-concept, adjustment and attitude towards both the groups. Second stage involves 'treatment' to the experimental group.

During this stage the experimental group teachers will employ the mastery learning strategy for teaching : and the teachers of the control group will use their conventional method of teaching. The time devoted in the teaching of Mathematics and Sicence will be controlled in both the group. Theird stage is the stage of the post testing. After the treatment is over, the cognitive and non-cognitive aspects of the personality of scheduled caste students will be measured.

Sample

20 Male teachers teaching Mathematics and Science to grade VI, matched on age, qualification, and experience, from school having similar conditions and context will be selected for the study. The sample of pupils will be incidental in the sense that the number will depend upon their presence in the classes taught by the teachers, sampled for the study.

Tools

The following tools will be used for study :

1. Cattell's Culture Fair Test of Mental Abilities to measure intelligence of pupils.
2. Kapoor soeio-economic status seale to measure socio-economic—status of popils.
3. A test measuring the self concept of pupils.
4. To measure attitude of popils towards Mathematics (to be developed).
5. To measure attitude of pupils towards science (to be developed).

Table-I

Design of the Study

No. Stage	*Duration*	*Treatment*	
		Control Gurop	*Experimental Group*
1. Pre-testing	Two Weeks	1. Administration of Mathematics achievement test. 2. Administration of Science Achievement test. 3. Administration of self-concept test. 4. Administration of adjustment inventory. 5. Administration of attitude scale.	1. Administration of Mathematics achievement test. 2. Administration of Sicence Achievement test. 3. Administration of self-concept test. 4. Administration of adjustment inventory. 5. Administration of attitude scale.
2. Treatment	36 weeks	Conventional Teaching	Teaching through Mastery Learning strategy
3. Post-testing	Two Weeks	Control Group 1. Administration of Mathematics achievement-test. 2. Administration of Science Achievement-test. 3. Administration of self-concept test. 4. Administration of adjustment inventory. 5. Administration of attitude scale.	Experimental Group 1. Administration of Mathematics Achievement test. 2. Administration of Science Achievement test. 3. Administration of self-concept test. 4. Administration of adjustment inventory 5. Administration of attitude scale.

The independent variable dependent veriables and the control varibales, with the kind of control employed in the study have been summarised in Table—II.

Table—II

Variables

Independent Variables	*Dependent Variables*	*Control*	
		Variables	*Controls employed*
Method of Teaching (Mastery Learing strategy and conventional	1. Achievement of pupils in Science.	1. Sex of Teacher.	Administrative (only male teacher will be selected)
	2. Achievement of pupils in Mathematics.	2. Grade to be taught	Administrative (only VI grade to be taught)
	3. Self-concept of pupils.	3. Subject to be taught	Administrative (Mathematics & Science to be taught)
	4. Adjustment of pupils.	4. Contamination between the Experimentals & control group teachers.	Administrative (Experimental & control groups in separate schools.)
		5. Hellow effect	Adminisirative (Ignorance about the experiment)
		6. Pupil's Intelligence	Statistical (Analysis of Covarience)
		7. Pupli's Socio-economic status.	Statistical (Analysis of Covarience)

6. Achievement test in Mathematics (to be developed).
7. Achievement test in Science (to be developed).
8. Pre-Adolescent Adjustment Inventory by Pareek and Rao.

Procedure

1. *Preparation of the Experimental Treatment Materials*

Instructional materials on the topics to be covered through M.L.S. alongwith Mastery tests will be prepared. A manual of direction for the teachers to use the material using different M.L.S. will also be developed.

2. *Preparing the teachers for Experimental Treatment*

All the ten teachers in Experimental group will be provided training in using Mastery Learning Strategy. For this purpose two week programme of training will be organised.

3. *Pre-testing*

The following tests will be administered in their respective order in both the experiemental and the control groups.

1. Intelligence test
2. Socio-economic status
3. Achievement tests in Mathematics
4. Achievement test in Science
5. Self-concept
6. Adjustment inventory
7. Attitude Scale.

4. *Administration of Experimental Treatment*

After administration of tests, teaching the decided content will be started immediately by all the teachers. The teachers in experimental group will be using mastery learcing strategy and teachers in control group will be using their conventional method of teaching.

5. *Post-testing*

The following tests will be administered to the pupils at this stage :

1. Achievement test in Mathematics
2. Achievement test in Science.
3. Self-concept test
4. Adjustment inventory
5. Attitude scale

6. *Analysis and Interpretation of Data*

(a) Analysis of covarience will be used for adjusting pupil's achievement in Mathematics and Science on intelligence and socio-economic—status of pupils.

(b) T-test will be used for fining the significance of difference between the adjusted means of different scores. T-test will also be used for testing the signifcancce of mean gain scores of the control and experimental groups.

Bibliography

Acharya, Anil Kumar : *Uplift of the Scheduled Castes and Tribes Plea for Planned Programme.* The Modern Review Vol. C XX-IX No. 4 Oct., 1971.

Adiseshiah, M.S., and Ramanathan, S. : *Educational Problem of Scheduled Castes and Tribes in Tamil Nadu.* Madras, Institute of Development Studies, 1974.

Aggarwal, R. : *A Study of Self Disclosure and Academic Achievement as related to Self-concept and Parent Child Relationship Among Major Castes with Special Reference to Girl Students,* Ph.D., Psy. Agra U., 1982.

Aggarwal, Partap, C. : *Equality through Privilege: A study of speical Privilege granted to the scheduled castes in Haryana* ICSSR, Research Abstracts, Quarterly Vol. II, No. 3 & 4, 1986.

Ahmed, N. : *Educational Opportunities and Socio-economic Changes Among the Muslim Backward Classes, Non-Muslim Backward classes and scheduled castes of Faizabad District during the Post-Independance Period, a Comparative Study* Ph.D. Edu, AMU, 1980.

Ahmed, Kaurna, Towards Equality : *Consequences of Protective Discrimination,* Economic and Political weekly 13, 2, 1978.

Aikara, J. : *Scheduled Castes and Higher Education—A Study of College Students in Bombay,* Unit of Research in Sociology of Education, Tata Institute of Social Sciences, Bombay, 1980.

Anumkampa, Rish : *A Comparative Study of the Vocational Aspiration of the Scheduled Caste Students with those of the non-scheduled Caste Students of Senior Secondary Schools of Delhi,* M.Ed. Dissertation Delhi Uni. 1982.

Ameerjan, H. S. : *Background Variables of the Scheduled Caste and Scheduled Tribe College Students—A Comprative Study*, Indian Educational Review, 19, 2, April 1984, 28-36.

Bariel, R.N.P.; *An Investigation into the Impact of Social Class Backward Upon Educational Achievement and Motivation*, Ph.D. Edu. Pat. U. 1966, A Survey of Research in Education edited by M.B. Buch, Serial No. 6.

Barkar, V.V. and Kurulkar, R.P. : *Post graduate Employment Experience of the Weaker Castes*, The Indian Institute of Education, Pune, 1982.

Block, J.H. : Introduction to Mastery Learning—Theory and Practice. (In J.H. Block ed). *Mastery Learning Theory and Practice* New York Holt, Renchord and Winston Inc., 1971.

Block, J.H. : Operating Procedure for Mastery Learning (In J.H. Block Ed.) *Mastery Learning—Theory and Practice* New York Holt, Rinchart and Winston Inc. 1971.

Bloom B.S. : *Stability and Changes in Human Characteristics* New York John Wiley and Sons, 1964.

Bloom B.S., : *Human Characteristics and School Learning* New York Mc Grow Hill, 1976.

Bloom, B.S., : Englehert, M. Furst E, Hill W and Krochwold *Taxonomy of Educational Objectives. The classification of Educational Goals Hand Book—1 Cognitive Domain* New York Longmans Green, 1956.

Bloom B.S., : *Mastery Learning and the Implications for Curriculum Development (In W. Ellort ed) In Confronting Curriculum Reform*, New York, 1971.

Bose, A.B., : *Plan Programmes for the Welfare of Scheduled* Castes, Social Welfare, Vol. XVI No. 1 and 2, 1969.

Bradburn, N.N., : "*n—Achievement and Father Dominance in Turkey*", Journal of Abnormal and Social Psychology, 1963, 67(5), 464-68.

Buch, M.B., : *A Survey of Research in Education* Faculty of Education and Psychology, M.S. University, Baroda, 1974.

Buch, M.B., : *Second Survey of Research in Education* (1972-78) Baroda Society for Educational Research and Development, 1979.

Burial, R.N.P., : *An Investigation into the Impact of Social Class Backward upon Educational Achievement and Motivation*, Ph.D. Edu. Pat. U. 1966.

Cameron, Ann and Storm, Thomas, : *Achievement Motivation in Canadian Indian, Middle and Working Class Children*, Psychological Report, Psychological Abstracts of 1965 at Serial No. 9913.

Carroil, J.B. Problem of Measurement related to the concept of learning for Mastery (In J.H. Blook ed.) *Mastery Learning and Practic.* New York Holt Rinchart and Wingston Inc, 1971.

Chand, Puran : *An Investigation into Vocational Aspiration of Scheduled Caste Students of Higher Secondary Classes in Delhi and their Relationship with Courses of offerings*, Delhi University, M.Ed. Dissertation (1974-75).

Chandersekharaih, K. : *Educational Problems of scheduled castes* Dharwar; Department of sociology, Karnataka University, 1969.

Chatterjee, B. : *School Dropout Among Harijan Children : Causes and Cure*, New Delhi; Central Inst tute of Research and Training in Public Cooperation, 1975.

Chaudhary, Saroj Kanti, : *Educational Progress in Rural Bengal* Economic and Politically Weekly, Vol. V. No. 6 Feb. 1970.

Chauhan, Brij Raj, : *Special Problems Regarding Education Among Scheduled Castes*, Papers in the sociology of Education in India (Ed.) Desai, I.P. Gore, M S. and Chitnis, S., New Delhi: NCERT., 1967.

Chauhan, B.R. and Narayan, G. : *Problems of Education Among Scheduled Castcs in Uttar Pradesh.* Social Change, Vol. 9 No. 1 and 2 March/June, 1976.

Chauhan, B.R. and others ; *Scheduled castes and Education Meerut* : Anu Publication, 1975.

Chitnis, Suma : *A Long Way to go, Report on a Survey of Scheduled Caste High School and College Students in Fifteen States of India.* Surat; Centre for Social Studies, 1977.

Chitnis, Suma : *Education for Equalitive : Case af Scheduled Castes in Higher Education,* Economic and Politically Weekly, Vol. VII Nos. 31-33, August, 1972.

Chitnis Suma : *Problems of Scheduled Caste College Students of Bombay* : Tata Institute of Social Sciences, 1976.

Chitnis, Suma : *Education of the scheduled castes* : Journal of Higher Education, Vo. I, No. 2 Autumn, 1975.

Chitra, M.N. : *The Social Background of Some Undergraduate Women Studies in Mysore City,* Ph.D. Soc. Del. U. 1969. A Survey of Research in Education, edited by M.B. Buch.

Choksi, Amita · *A Study of Achievement Motivation, Adjustment, Academic Motivation, Anxiety in Relation to Sex and Socio-economic Background of Pupils of Nine Standard of the English Medium School of Baroda.* M.Ed., Dissertation, CASE, Baroda.

Commissioner *for Scheduled Castes and Scheduled Tribes,* 1971-72 and 1972-73 Ministry of Education and Culture, New Delhi Government of India, 1980.

Dantawala : *M.L. Social Dimension of Poverty,* Vishleshan, Vol. II, No. 2, June, 1976.

Desai, I.P. and Pandor, G.A. : *The scheduled caste and Tribe His school students in Gujarat,* Surat : Centre for Regions Development studies, 1974.

D'souza, V.S. : *Educational Inequalities Among Scheduled Castes a Case Study in the Puajab,* Deptt. of Soc., Pan. U., 1980 (ICSSR Financed).

Dubey, S.N., and Mathur Usha : *Welfare Programme for scheduled castes, contents and Administration,* Economic and Political Weekly, VII, 4, 1972.

Dubey, S.M. : *Study af scheduled caste and scheduled Tribe students of Assam* (Vol. I—school). Dibrugarh Department of sociology and centre for sociological study of the forntier region, 1974.

Dubey, S.M. : *Study of Scheduled Caste and Scheduled Tribe students in Assam (Volume II)*. Department of Sociology and Centre for Sociological Study of the Frontier Region, 1974.

Eleaner, R.H. : *Motivation and Achievement in Black and White Junior College Students*, Vol. 97 First Half Oct., 1975. The Journal of Social Psychology, p. 107-113.

Gandrade, K.D. : *Educational Problems of Scheduled Castes in Haryana* (School Students), Delhi: Delhi schools of social work, 1974.

Gangrade, K.D. : *Educational Problems of the scheduled castes in Haryana* (College students), Delhi : Delhi school of social work, 1974.

Garrentt, E. Henry : *Statistics in Psychology and Education*, Dovid Mckay Company Inc., New York, 1926.

Gaur, J.S. and Others : *Psychological Basis of Educational and Vocational Development of Scheduled Caste Students*. NCERT ERIC Project, New Delhi 1987.

George, E.I. : *Educational Problems of the scheduled castes and Tribes College students in Kerala Trivendrum* : Departt. of Psychology University of Kerala, 1975.

Gakulnathan, P.P. : *A study of Achievement Related to Motivation (n—Achievement and Anxiety) and Educational Achievement Amang Secondary School Pupils*, Ph.D. Edu. Del. U. 1972.

Gore, G.M. : *Socio-Economic Study of the Scheduled Castes in Rural Maharashtra*, I.C.S.S.R. Research Abstracts Quarterly, New Delhi : Orient Longman, Vol. III, No. 2 & 3 Jan.-April, 1974.

Goyal, S.K. : *The study of scheduled caste students of college in East U.P.*, Varanasi : Department of sociology, Banaras Hindu University, 1974.

Gupta, L.P. : *Vocational Choices of Scheduled & Non-Scheduled Caste Students*, *EPA Bulletin*, Vol. 5 No. 2, July, 1982, 47-51.

Guilford, J.P. : *Fundamental Statistics in Psychology and Education*, New Delhi, Tokyo McGraw Hill, Koga Kusha U, 1897.

Hines, George H.: *Motivational Correlates of Pacific Islands in Urban Environment*, Journal of Psychology March, 1973, Vol. 89, p. 247-249.

Husen T. : *International Study of Educational Achievement in Mathematics. A comparision of twelve countries* Vol. I and II New York John Willey and sons, 1967.

Hussan, Amir : *Harijan Welfare in Uttar Pradesh*, Special Welfare, Vol. XVIII, No. 10, January, 1972.

Indian Institute of Psychometry, : *Comparison of the Proformance of the Scheduled Caste and Scheduled Tribe candidates in Aptitude and Knowledge Test with that of General candidates*, Calcutta, 1982.

Jangira, N.K. : *Universal Learning Strategy for Primary School.* The Primary Teacher Vol. V No. 1 Jan. pp. 20, 1980.

Jangira, N.K. : *Teacher Training and Teacher Effectiveness—An Experiment in Teacher Education.* New Delhi National Publishing House, 1979.

Jha, M.L. : *Untouchability and Education, Meerut : Namita* Publications, 1973.

Joshi, S.D. : *Educational Problems of the Scheduled Castes and Scheduled Tribes of Baroda District*, Ph.D. Edu., M.S.U., 1980.

Julka, G.L. : *Aggression, Fear and Anxiety in Children (their educational implication)* Ph.D. Edu. Raj. U., 1963.

Kamlesh, A. : *A Comparative Study of Self Concept, Adjustment, Interests and Motivation among the scheduled caste and Non-scheduled caste students*, Ph. D. Edu., Kan. U., 1981.

Karlekar, Malvika : *Higher Education and the Scheduled Castes* Journal of Higher Education, Vol. I, No. 2, Autumn, 1975.

Kaul, V. : *A Study of Some Congitive and Socio-emotional Variables With respect to Socio-ecomomically Disadvantaged Children*, Ph. D. Psy., IIT, Delhi 1982.

Kedetotad, N.K. : *Religion and Society Among the Harijans A Quarterely Journal of Indian Dissertation.* Vol. VI No. I Jan-March, 1987 ICSSR New Delhi.

Kersh Mildred E. : A Strategy for Mastery Learning in fifth grade Arithmatic (In J.H. Block ed.). *Mastery Learning Theogy and Practic New York Holt Rinchart and Winston Inc.*, 1970.

Khattri, P.K. : *Reduction of Abusive Behaviour as a Function of Types of Reinforcement and Awareness in Socially Disadvantaged Children*, Ph. D. Psy., Inc., U., 1979.

Khobragade, N.T. and Patel, P. R. : *Review of Admissions and Parformance of Backward Class Students in a Polytechnic Government Prtiechnic*, Delhi, 1981.

Khurana, G. : *Educational Facilities for scheduled castes.* The Educational Quarterely. Vol. XXXI, Numbers 3&4, Ministery of Education and Social Welfare, Government of India, October, 1979 and January, 1980.

Kim Hogwon et. al : *A study of the Bloom Strategy for Mastery Learning.* (In J.H. Block Ed) Mastery Learning Theogy and Practice New York Holt Rinchart and Winston Inc., 1969.

Kirpal, Viney : *Higer Education for the Scheduled Castes and Scheduled Tribes*, Economic and Political Weekly, 13, 4 & 5, 1978.

Lakshanna, C. : *The Study of Scheduled Castes and Scheduled Tribe School Students in Andhra Prades*, Hyderabad Department of Sociology, Osmania University, 1974.

Lal, Sheo Kumar, : *Educational Progress and Problems of Scheduled Castes and Tribes College students in Andhra Pradesh*, Hyderabad. Deptt. of Sociology, Osmania University, 1974.

Lal, Sheo Kumar : *Educational Progress and Problems of Scheduled Castes and Scheculed Tribes College Students, in Rajasthan.* The University of Jodhpur, Jodhpur, 1974.

Lal, Shayam, : *Caste and Occupationol Mobility in a Jodhpur Bhangi Bustee*, Journal of Social Research, 18, 2, 1975.

Laxmidevi : *The Study of the Problems of Child Development Among the Harijans of Gujarat*, Ph. D. Soc., Work, Gujarat Vidyapith, Ahmedabad 1980.

Malik, Suneila, *Social Integration of scheduled castes*, New Delhi : Abhinav Publications, 1979.

Malik, Suneila : *Social Consequences of Social Mobility Among Scheduled Castes.* Ph. D. Theses Chandigarh, Punjab University, 1981.

Maurya, Ram Lal : *Status and Role of Scheduled Caste in Rural India,* Ph. D. Thesis, Lucknow : Lucknow University 1976.

Mehta Paryag : "*Level of n. Ach In High School Boys*" Indian Educational Review, 1967, 2 (2) 36—70.

Mehta Prayag : *Socio—Psychological Interventions for Universalising Education, A case for radical social transformation and non-formal education,* New Delhi : National Labour Institute, 1976.

Ministry of Education and Social Welfare : *National Policy on Education.* MHRD, Govt. of India New Delhi, 1986.

Ministry of Educational and Culture, *Educational Statistics at Glance*, New Delhi, MEC, 1983.

Ministry of Education : *Report of the Education Commission (1964-66).* MOE, Govt. of India, New Delhi, 1966.

Ministry of Education : *National Policy on Education* Ministry of Education, Govt. of India Publication No. 832, New Delhi, 1968.

Ministry of Education : *Secondary Education Commission (1952-1953) Ministry of Education* Govt. of India Delhi, 1953.

Minigione, Anne, D. ; "*Need for Achievement in Negro White and Pure to Rican Children* Journal of Consulting and Clinical Psychology, 1978, 32 (i) 94-95 as abstracted in the Psychological Abstracts of 1968. 1 Serial No. 7353.

Mishra, Yogendra Nath : *Educational Adaptation. Social Ambition and Performance of Scheduled Caste Students at the Various Educational Levels in the Rewa District of* Madhya Pradesh, Rewa : Govt. of Education, (M.P.) 1978.

Mishra, Shashikanth : *Steeling the Harijana Samanvaya Ashram*, People's Action, India, (M), December, 1973.

Nagaraju, G.S. : *A Study of a Few Social Factors Affecting Scholastic Achievements of Scheduled Caste Students Studying in Secondary Schools of Karnataka*, Ph. D. Ed. Banglore Uni., 1977.

Naid V.S. : "Self-image of Scheduled Caste Educated Youth" *Indian Journal of Social Work*, Vol. XL, II, No. 2, July 1982, 149-154.

Naik, J.P : *Education of the Scheduled Castes (1965-66)*. ICSSR Occasional Monogrpaph, New Delhi : The Caxton Press Private Limited, 1971.

Nayer, P.K.B. : *The Scheduled Caste and Tribe High School Students in Kerala*, Trivendrhm: Department of Sociology, University of Kerala, 1975.

Nautiyal, K.C. and Sharma, Y.D. : *Equalisation of Educational Opportunities for scheauled castes and scheduled Tribes* : New Delhi, NCERT, 1979.

Pandey, P.N. : *Education and Social Mobility Among Scheduled Castes*, Ph. D. Soc., BHU, 1979.

Parkash, Om : *A Study of Some Psycho-social Variables among caste Hindu and Scheduled Caste Children in the Rural Set-up*, Ph. D. Psy., Del U., 1981.

Parvathama, C. : *A study of the Scheduled Caste and Scheduled Tribe College Students in Karnataka*. Mysore Deptt. of Post-Graduate Studies and Research in Sociology, 1974.

Parmar, Yohan A. : *The Mahyavanshi : A study of a scheduled Caste in Surat City*, Ph. D. Thesis, Surat south Gujrat University, 1978.

Patwardhan, Sunanda : *Change Among India's Harijans : Maharashtra. A case study* New Delhi : Orient Longman, 1973.

Pathak, K.D. : *Anusuchit Joti Awam Janajati Ke Vidyesthiyon Ki Akanksha aur Abhivrittyatmak Unmukhata Main Pariwarten (Changes in Attitudinal Orientation and Aspiration of scheduled caste and scheduled tribes students)* Ph.D. Soc, BHU, 1981.

Pendharkar, Y : *Occupational Aspiration of the Students upto Undergraduate level (with special reference to the Hindu Studehts of the City of Indore)*, Ph. D. Soc, Indore U., 1977.

Pimpley, P.N. : *Educational Problems of scheduled caste students in the Punjab (College students)*, Chandigarh : Department of sociology Punjab University, 1974.

Pimpley, P.N. : *The Problem of Non-attendance of school of the children of the Scheduled Castes in Haryana*, Chandigaarh : Deptt. Sociology : Punjab Univ. 1978.

Pimpley P.N. and Kapoor, Bushan Lal : *Educational Problems of Female Scheduled Castes Students in Punjab, Interdescipline* Vol. 12 No. 2 & 3, Winter, 1975.

Pimplay, P.N. : *Educational Problems of scheduled castes in Punjab* : (school students, Chandigarh Department of sociology, 1974.

Pimplay, P.N., and Kapoor, Bushan Lal: *Educational Problems of female scheduled caste students in Punjab*, Interdescripline, Vol. 12 No. 2 and 3, Wintar, 1975.

Pisharody, K.G.S. : *Organisation and Administration of welfare Programme for Backward classes*, The Indian Journal of social work, Vol. XXXIII No. 1, April, 1972.

Poussaint Aluin F & Atkinson, : Cardyn (Tuft U. Medical School) "*Negro Youths and Psychological Motivation*" Journal of Negro Education, 1968 (Sum) Vol. 37 (3) 241-257.

Prajapati, G.K. : *Impact of Education on Social, Economic and Political changes Among Scheduled Castes, a study of Danapore sub-division*, Ph. D. Edu., Pat U, 1982.

Premi, K.K. : *Educational Opportunities for the Scheduled Castes : Role of Protective Discrimination in Equalisation*, Ph. D. Edu : New Delhi : Jawahar Lal University, 1977.

Punalekar, S.P. : *School Dropout Among Harijan Children. Causes and Cure. New Delhi : Central Institute of* Research and Training in Public Cooperation, 1975.

Rajagopalan, C. : *Educational Progress and Problem of Scheduled Caste and Scheduled Tribe Students in Karanataka* (High School) Bangalore : Deptt. of Sociology, Banglore University, 1974.

Ramanamma, A. and Bambawale, Usha : *Sociological Implication of School Dropouts in Maharashtra, social* change., 8, 2, 1978.

Ramaswamy, Uma : *Scheduled Castes in Andhra : Some Aspects of social* change, Economic and Political Weekly, 1974.

Ramaswamy, Uma : *Self indentiy Among scheduled castes : A study of Andhra,* Economic and Political Weekly, 9, 47, 1974.

Ram, Nandu : *Bridging the gap Between the scheduled caste and Non-scheduled castes,* the Journal of social Transformation, Vol. 3. No. 2-3, June-September, 1979

Ramdhan : *Safequards for Harijans still Inadequate* Mainstream, sixteen Annual Number, 1978.

Rangari, A.D., : *Comparative Study of the Scheduled Castes and the Non-Scheduled Caste College Students of Aurangabad,* Ph. D. Psy. Poona U., 1981.

Rani B. : "*Self Concept and other Non-cognitive Factors Affecting the Academic Achivement of the Scheduled Caste Students in the Institutions for Higher Technical Education*" Deptt. of Education, Ph. D. JNU, 1981.

Rastogi, Shital Prasad : *The Impact of constitutional Provisions upon the uplift of Harijans* Ph.D. Thesie, Lucknow University, 1976.

Rath R. and Misra S.K. : *The study of scheduled caste and scheduled Tribe College students in Orissa,* Bhubaneswar, Deptt. of Psychology, Utkal University, 1974.

Rath R. Dash S. and Dash V.N. : *Cognitive Abilities and School Achievements of the Socially Disadvantaged Children in Primary School.* Bombay Allied Publication Pvt. Ltd., 1979.

Sachchidanand : *Education Among the Scheduled Caste and Schnduled Tribes in Bihar* (School Students), A.N.S. Institute of Social Studies, Patna, 1974.

Sachchidanand : *Education Among the scheduled castes and scheduled Tribes in Bihar* (College Students), A.N.S. Institute of Social studies Patna, 1974.

Sahai, K.M. : *Towards People's Participation in Social Welfare* Programmes, Prashasnika Vol. VII No. 3-4 July-Dec., 1978, 44-49.

Santha Kumari R. : *Impact of Welfare Measure on the Backward Classes : A Study of the Scheduled Castes of Kerala*, Ph. D. Thisis, Trivendrum : University of Kerala, 1976.

Sapra, C.L. : *Educational Wastage and Stagnation in India*, NCERT, New Delhi 1967.

SCERT : *Career and Placement Study of Scheduled Castes and Scheduled Tribes Students in Selected District of Tamil Nadu* (1974-76) Madras, 1979.

Sen A. : *Identity Formation and Self Identity of the Harijans Elite*, Deptt. of Edu., Kal. Uni., 1982 (ICSSR Financed).

Shah, Ghanshayam : *Politics of Scheduled Castes and Tribes* : Bombay Vora and Co., 1975. Reviewed by H.N. Singh in Sociological Bulletin, 24, 2, 1975, 234-235, quoted from ICSSR Journal of Abstracts and Reviews Vol. 5, No. 2 Jul-Dec., 1976 New Delhi.

Shah, V.P. and Patel, Tara : *Who goes to College*? Ahmedabad: Rachana Prakashan, 1977 (Reviewed by V. Eswara Reddy in social change, 8, 1, 1978.

Shah. B.P. and Thaker, J.D. : *Education Problem of Scheduled Caste and Scheduled Tribes College Students in Gujarat*. Department of Sociology, Vallabh Vidyanagar, Sardar Patel University, 1974.

Shivashankara, H.V. : *A Study of Psychological Factors and Academic Achivement of the Socially Disadvantaged* Ph.D. Psy. Kar. U., 1981.

Shantha Kumari, R. : *Impact of Welfare Measure on the Backwark classes : A study of the scheduled castes of Kerala*. Ph. D. Thesis, Trivendrum University of Kerala, 1976.

Sharma, G.B. : *Machinery for the Administration of Welfare Programme for Backward Classes at the state level*. The Indian Journal of Public Administration, Vol. XXII, No. 3, July-Sept., 1976.

Sharma, J.P. : *A Study of Scheduled Caste Students in Patna University*, Ph.D. Edu. Pat. U., 1982.

Sharma, M.C. : *A Psychological Study of Adjustment Problems of Harijans and Backward Class Students of Agra Distt.* Ph. D. Psy. Agra U. 1979.

Sharma, R.C. and Sapra, C.L. : *Westage ana Stagnation in Primary and Middle Schools in India.* New Delhi, N.C.E.R.T., 1969.

Singh, J.P. and Others : *The Study of the Scheduled Castes and Tribes Students of Scondary Schools in U.P.* Department of Economics, Ghandian Institute of studies, March, 1974.

Singh, M. : *Social Origins, Educational Attainments and Occupatianal Mobility Among Scheduled Castes in Delhi,* Ph.D. Soc. So, JNU, 1980.

Singh R.P. : *Inter Caste Differences Among the Scheduled Castes in Achievement at Secondary Stage of Education* NCERT (ERIC Project) New Delhi, 1986.

Singh R.P. : *Educational Backwardness of Scheduled Caste Students and Need-Oriented Plan for their Development.* Deptt. of Edu., Pat. U., 1982.

Singh, S.N., : *A Study of the Pattern of Education and Occupation of Patterns living in Varanasi (Rural with Special Reference of Scheduled Castes,* ICSSR Research Abstracts, Quarterly New Delhi : Orient Longman, Vol. III, No. 2. and 3, Jan.-April, 1974.

Signh, T.P. and Others : *The Study of Scheduled Castes and Tribe Students of Secondary Schools in U.P.* Deptt. of Economic Gandhian Institute of studies, 1974.

Singh, Narender Kumar: *Educational Problems of the Scheduled Caste and Scheduled Tribe Students in Rajasthan.* University Department of Sociology University of Rajasthan Jaipur, 1975.

Soni, B.D. : *Educational Problems of Scheduled Caste College Students in U.P. (West)* Research Report, Agra, Department of Sociology, Institute of Social Sciences, 1975 (ICSSR sponsored.

Soni, B.D. : *Educational Problems of Scheduled Caste College Students in U.P. East* Research Report, Agra, Deptt. of sociology Institute of social science, 1975.

Sukhia, S.P. aud Others : *Elements of Educational Research* Allied Publishers Delhi, 1963.

Sutradhar, P.K. : *Socially Disadvantaged and Advantaged Children : a Psychological Study of their Relative Academic Achievement*, Ph. D. Applied Psy. Cal. U., 1982.

Toha, M. and S.A.C. ; Changing Values Among Untouchables Through Education. *Indian Education Review*, Volume VI, No. 2, New Delhi, N.C.E.R.T.. July, 1971.

Trivedi, S.R. : *Experiences and Problems About Education of Scheduled Castes Hostellers in sagar* Vanyajati, Vol. XXV No. 4, Oct., 1977.

Tribhuvan, V.D. : *A Study of Educated Scheduled Caste Women in an Urban Setting*, Ph. D. Soc, Poona U., 1975.

UNESCO : *Educational Westage in Development Digest*, USAID Vol. VI No. 1 January 1968 p. 75.

Uniyal, M.P. and Shah, B.: *Study of Caste-effect Upon Various Academic Areas at Graduate Level of Kumaun University*, Deptt. of Education, Kum., U., 1979.

Upadhyay, H.C. : *The Problems of Scheduled Castes in the Kumaun Hills : a sociological study*, Ph.D. Soc. Kum. U., 1981.

Ushasri, S.A., : *A Comparative Study of the Socially Disadvantaged and the Socially non-disadvantaed Pupils with regards to Scholastic Achievement and Academic Adjustment*, Ph. D. Psy. SU. U., 1978.

Vagiswaoi, A. : *Status and Earning Trands of Tamil Nadu Harijan* ICSSR Research Abstracts. Quarterly New Delhi : Orient Longman Vol. II, No. 4, July, 1973.

Valunjkar, T.N. : *Educational Problems of the Scheduled Caste and Scheduled Tribe Secondary School Students in Maharashtra*, Nagpure, Deptt. of Sociology, 1975.

Vidyavathi, P.R. : *A Study of Ethnic Group Influences on Socialization of Primary School Children in the age-group 8-12 years in the city of Mysore*, Ph.D. Thesis, University of Mysore, Mysore, 1974.

Vyas, Harendra, : *Scheduled Castes-Some Problems and solutions* Vanyajati, Vol. XVI, No. 2, April. 1968.

Yadav, P.S. : *Effect of Mastery Learning Strategy in Pupil Achievement in Mathematics*. Doctoral Work Kurukshetra University, Kurushetra, 1981.

Yadav, Satish Kumar : *Harijan Awareness of Educational Schemes for Scheduled Castes*, Gurgaon, Academic Press, 1983.

Yadav, Satish Kumar : *Educational of Scheduled Castes : Problems and Solution*, Avaghana : Vol. 3, No. 1, April, 1979.

Yadav, Satish Kumar : *Intelligence, Motivational Tendencies of Scheduled Castes and non-scheduled Caste Secondary Students*, Journal of education and Psychology, Vol. XX, No. 15, 1979.

Yadav, S.K. : *Attitude Scale Towards Games and Sports*, R.C.E. Ajmer, 1976.

Yadav, S.K., *A Study of Scheduled Castes Awareness About Schemes for their Educational Progress* Ph D. Thesis, M.S.U., Baroda, 1981.

Yadav Satish Kumar : *Education of Scheduled Castes : Problems and Solutions*, Avaghana : Vol. 3, No. 1, April, 1979.

Radav, S.K. : *Educational Schemes for Scheduled Castes : Teachers Perception Profile* Gurgaon, Book Worto. 1685

Index